THE
SHEPHERD

THE
SHEPHERD

ROGER DIXON

authorHOUSE®

AuthorHouse™
1663 Liberty Drive
Bloomington, IN 47403
www.authorhouse.com
Phone: 1-800-839-8640

First published by AuthorHouse   02/02/2012

ISBN: 978-1-4678-8482-2 (sc)
ISBN: 978-1-4678-8481-5 (ebk)

By the same Author

The Messiah —

Going to Jerusalem — Both originally published by Collins Publishers, London

Noah II — in collaboration with Basil Bova

Christ on Trial — also with Basil Bova
— both originally published by Ace Books of New York

Christ on Trial was serialised in the London Sunday Express

I dedicate this book to my lifelong friend and collaborator Basil Bova without whose inspiration and encouragement I would never have attempted it—and much else!

Prologue

The fishermen on the beach were the first to see them, or rather a small girl who had come to see her father and two elder brothers set out.

She had wanted to come too, but her brothers laughed at her and told her to go home to their mother where she belonged, so she was kicking the side of the boat in frustration while looking out to sea.

The others were busy getting their newly mended nets into the boat and the sun was still hidden behind the mountains behind them, but the eastern sky was red, turning to orange and a few minutes would see its first rays strike across the bay.

Patches of white on the horizon caught her eye but at first no one took any notice when she told them. But eventually her father, who was a Levite and so the head of the village paused in his work and looked in the direction she was pointing.

'What is it Ruth?'

'It looks like a flock of sea gulls floating towards us, father.'

The man stared more intently then drew the attention of his sons.

'Those aren't birds—they're ships'

The one called Etham frowned. They are ships . . . but bigger than I've ever seen.

They watched in silence as what were now quite clearly large vessels approaching and could not now be more than two miles off shore.

'There's a lot more behind them' the younger brother said, and both boys looked at their father. 'They're going to land on the beach.!' By now the other boat owners had stopped what they were doing and were all staring in the same direction as the ships in front could be seen lowering their main sails and continuing more slowly.

The first rays of the sun rising behind them revealed the full extent of the approaching fleet and now, for the first time they saw the flash of what could only be weapons in the hands of those manning the gunnels ready to leap ashore. Weapons, none of them had ever seen before.

Suddenly the Levite turned and shouted at those on the beach with him.

'Leave everything. Get back to the village and prepare to hide in the forest until we see their intentions.'

Everyone turned to escape, the Levite sweeping Ruth up into his arms before running inland with the others.

Only Etham did not follow. His curiosity getting the better of him, he climbed a tree at the edge of the sand to watch the landing.

He saw the leading vessels come to a halt about twenty yards off shore and at once dozens of men jumped into the water with ropes to pull the ships closer to the beach while others, carrying what looked like shiny sticks, scrambled on to the beach and stood in a semi circle as if to ward off an expected attack.

As soon as the leading ships were secure, doors in the bows were lowered and men led horses forward and tied them to the trees bordering the beach, one of them to the tree where Etham was hiding.

During the course of the morning, the ships at the rear were brought in until they lined the sea shore and men and supplies were disembarked until the beach was covered with supplies and men and horses wheeled in all directions, evidently according to some pre-arranged plan.

After a few hours some of the men saddled horses and rode out of sight in land and Etham only hoped his family and the others had escaped up into the mountains in time.

Some of the fishermen's boats were broken up and large fires started on which food was cooked but one who was obviously in authority shouted at those who had done so. Etham could not understand what was said but no more boats were destroyed after that.

Finally, two men with two hunting dogs each on leashes walked up the beach towards Etham's tree. It seemed they would walk on past, but the nearest whined and started to drag his handler until they were at the foot of the tree with all the dogs now wagging their tails and barking as they looked up into the tree.

One drew his shining stick and shouted up to where Etham was hiding. He did not understand what the man said, but it did not take much to guess what he wanted and climbed down.

The man stared at him with a half smile on his face and spoke in a normal voice, but Etham suddenly turned on his heel and ran. But he was no match for the dogs who brought him down and stood over him slobbering and wagging their tails until the two handlers arrived. One poked him with his stick which proved to have a sharp point until he stood up and, following his captors gestures, walked in front of them and up a gang plank into the heart of one of the ships.

He was pushed up to the top deck where a man seemed to be giving orders to the others.

He stopped as soon as he saw Etham and after the handlers had spoken to him they turned and left.

The leader looked around the group and said something, at which point one of the others, older than the rest spoke to him directly in his own language but heavily accented.

The interrogation took longer than it would have done but for the necessity of the leader's questions and Etham's subsequent answers having to be translated, but at the end of it Etham understood he would not be harmed if he behaved himself and did not try to escape, and the leader had learned that this was Canaanite country on the fringe of the Egyptian Empire which stretched as far as the Nile to the south.

Some food and water were brought to him and while he was eating this the leader, who now told Etham his name was Philistine, sat with him and through the interpreter told him they had come from an island far to the west which had been part of another Empire as great as that of Egypt and with skills far more advanced. But a volcanic eruption had forced the survivors to set out in as many ships as had been spared—not enough for more than a quarter of the population.

'What happened to those left behind?' Etham asked.

'They are probably dead by now' Philistine told him. 'There was nothing we could do.' He then questioned Etham, apparently casually, about the country where they had landed and its people and the young man assured him that their customs made it an obligation to offer hospitality to strangers. He was sure that when his father and the others were made aware of the circumstances which had caused the new arrivals to seek shelter they would be welcomed. Only a few hundred years ago his own people, the Israelites, had settled here having escaped from slavery in Egypt. It was a fertile land with not many people so there was plenty of room for the new comers. If they would let him seek out his father and talk to him, he was sure he could persuade him to come and meet them.

Philistine paused for a moment, then he nodded and stood up

'I will speak to my companions', he said., 'But what you suggest sounds a good idea'.

Soon afterwards, Etham was released, and went in search of his father and the others.

They were sceptical to begin with, but Etham was persuasive, and what he had told Philistine about the obligation of hospitality was true. It was agreed that his father and some other elders would go to meet the newcomers while the rest of them remained where they were until the outcome of the meeting was known.

Philistine welcomed the villagers warmly and a feast was prepared that went on for many hours with women and girls who had previously remained in the ships emerging to serve them. Later one of the younger girls danced for them to the music of instruments that were strange but produced a mysterious air that captivated the guests, particularly Etham, who was the only young man who had been allowed to accompany the elders.

Philistine smiled when he saw the boys eyes glued to the sensuous movements of the young dancer, and when her performance was over, asked him if he would like to take her back to his village as a gift. And seeing their puzzled looks, he laughed and said 'I did not mean to marry her. She is only a slave; my property as it happens. I give her to you to do as you like.!'

His companions laughed at this, but when it was translated Etham's father replied with as much tact as he could muster, to explain that having been in bondage in Egypt themselves, there was no place in their society for slaves.'

'Philistine frowned and the visitors wondered if he was offended. But then his smile returned and he said: 'I have already given her to your son so I cannot take her back. But if he likes, he can give her freedom, then she can choose whether to go with him or stay with us.'

The Levite nodded with some relief. 'That sounds a good solution. On behalf of my son, I thank you. But let the girl remain here. Etham is too young to be married.' What he did not say was that it was strictly forbidden by the Law of Moses for any Israelite to marry outside the faith.

Philistine nodded. Then he turned to one of the serving women and gave an order, following which, the girl was led forward into the firelight and Philistine explained to her that following his gift of her to their young visitor, he had granted her freedom, but she was to remain with them.

Her reaction was not at all what the Ethan and the others were expecting. She looked terrified and flung herself at his feet with a burst of pleading none of them could understand but took to be disappointment not to be coming with them. Philistine glanced at the women who had brought her forward and they dragged her to her feet, still wailing.

'Are you sure you will not change your mind' Philistine asked. Ethan's father glanced at his son. Their eyes met for a few seconds, then he turned back to their host and nodded.

'I am afraid so.'

'Very well' Philistine gestured again at the two women, who then dragged the girl away, before turning to his own men and murmuring, 'I am sure we have a role for her!'

This was not translated and Levite did not ask, but he saw a strange look pass between the ones his host had spoken too.

Realising his guests were mystified by the girl's behaviour, Philistine called for more wine to be served, but shortly after exchanging a few words with his companions, Levite rose to his feet to thank their hosts for their hospitality and suggested that they would be honoured if Philistine and his people would like to come to their village in a week's time so their friendship might be further encouraged. In the interval they would invite the people of other villages to join them in offering a suitable welcome.

After the Israelites had gone, a huge wooden statue was unloaded from one of the ships and set up on the beach. A large stone was dragged in front of it and when more wood had been thrown on newly lit fires, everyone from the ships gathered round as a priest stepped forward and began to intone prayers to Dagon the god of the Philistines whom the priest praised in a loud voice for bringing them safely to a new land.

The musicians began to play again, and once more the priest raised his voice.

'Great is the god Dagon who has provided for himself a sacrifice!'

Everyone fell silent as a naked young woman was led forward by two men—the young dancer who had been rejected by the Israelites—but now without protest and seemingly in a trance. When they reached the stone she allowed herself to be stretched out on it and closed her eyes.

The priest stepped forward again, this time carrying a long knife which he plunged into the girl's body. She died without a sound and her blood ran over the stone to drip down the sides.

'Great is Dagon and worthy of sacrifice' intoned the priest for the last time.

Then, without another word the onlookers turned and walked away, except for the two men who picked up the still graceful body of the girl, threw her onto the nearest fire.

On the date set, Philistine and his men rode into the village having been guided by Ethram who had been sent back to act as guide.

It was as his father had promised. Not only had all his own people returned but hundreds of others from neighbouring villages to welcome the new comers.

A feast began during which the Levite sat with Philistine and his chief men at a place of honour together with the elders from all the nearby villages.

When wine had been drunk, one of these got to his feet and made a speech of welcome which was translated for the benefit of the many guests. After this, Philistine rose to his feet. But before making a response he looked round and asked if everyone from the other villages was present, and when the elders replied that it was so—even the women and children who did not want to be missed out!

The Israelites chuckled at this as it was a joke that their women were of strong character who over the years had achieved near equality with their husbands and brothers.

Philistine glanced round at those who and come with him and nodded and these too rose to their feet.

Unsuspecting, the villagers watched with interest waiting perhaps for some gesture of friendship. What they got was very different:

Philistine swiftly drew his sword and with a single blow, decapitated the elder sitting next to him. His followers also drew their swords and within minutes all the men who had come to meet them were dead, including the Levite. The women were corralled into a huddled, weeping mass except for a few of the braver ones who had flung themselves at those butchering their men folk and who had also been cut to pieces.

A few of the younger women ran to escape as well as some of the men and boys. Several Philistines who had brought horses with them would have set off in pursuit, but Philistine called them back, shouting: 'Let them go. Let what happened here become known as a warning to any who try to oppose us!'

Etham and his brother had been dragged into a stable by their mother but they were soon discovered by a Philistine soldier who knocked the woman to the ground then ran the younger brother through with his sword. He was about to do the same to Ethram when he recognised him and dragged him over to where Philistine was standing with his sword in his right hand dripping with blood. The soldier threw the boy down in front of him.

'I thought you would like to see this one,' he boasted.

Philistine nodded and indicated with his sword that Etham should stand up.

The two looked at each other, then the older man said 'You should have had the girl while you had the chance' and with that he ran his sword into his body so hard the tip came out of his back.

For a brief second Etham stared in disbelief, then fell to the ground dead.

Philistine looked down for a second, then he barked 'Throw him on the fire. Perhaps they will meet in Hades!'

The calm of death reigned. The women eventually silenced by the enormity of what had happened.

Philistine called out to his men: 'Those who do not have a woman on the ships have first choice, but be careful with them until you feel they can be trusted. We need breeding stock if we are to survive.

Many of the younger men stepped forward as well as a few older ones and in a short space of time most of the younger women had been chosen and led away leaving about twenty who were either old or ugly.

Then Philistine called out again: 'Are you sure no one wants any of these?'

This was greeted by silence.

'Very well. We haven't enough food to waste . . . kill them!'

Chapter One

F ive hundred years had passed since Moses led the twelve
tribes out of slavery in Egypt. Although some remained
faithful to the Covenant revealed to them on Mount Sinai,
many had fallen away from the worship of the God of Abraham,
and in total disobedience to the laws Moses had given them,
intermarried with the pagan peoples who had remained after
the Israelites crossed the Jordan and occupied the Promised
Land, and joined with them in the worship of local gods such as
the Baals, which was far less demanding and promoted revelry
and general debauchery. As result, they lost the unity which
had enabled leaders such as Joshua to lead them to success.

Occasionally, other leaders, such as Gideon, arose to rescue
them from the domination of the surrounding nations who
constantly oppressed them, but as soon as these died, the tribes
fell back into their old ways and were soon as badly off as ever.

Then a new and more frightening threat arose. The
Philistines, a war like people of Greek origin. Armed with steel
swords and spears these easily established dominance over the
nearer Israelite tribes who had nothing to equal the weapons
brought against them, and the invaders made sure this state of

affairs continued by forbidding everyone else from working in iron and steel so that even simple agricultural tools had to be taken to Philistine blacksmiths for sharpening or repair.

Occasionally, the Israelites would rise up against their oppressors, but mostly with disastrous consequences, culminating with the capture of their most venerated symbol, the holy Ark itself which had been carried through the desert from Mount Sinai and contained the tablets on which they believed God himself had written the Ten Commandments.

Then a young priest arose; Samuel. Under his influence most of the tribes put aside their pagan idols and united under his leadership. The Philistines started to lose some battles and the Ark was recovered, but they remained in the new cities of Ashdod, Gath and Ekron on the coast as a constant threat.

But as Samuel became older, the tribes became uneasy. His sons showed no signs of having either the will or integrity to take his place and the people began to ask, why should they not have a King to go out and fight their battles for them like other nations?

This displeased Samuel greatly. The very thing that distinguished them from other peoples was the acceptance of Yahweh—the God of Israel, as their true king, ruling through prophetic leaders such as Samuel himself. He prayed to the Lord in anger, but after he had fallen into a sleep of exhaustion he dreamt that the Lord spoke to him

'Listen to all that the people are saying to you; it is not you they have rejected but me as their king—as they have done from the day I brought them up out of Egypt until this day, forsaking me and serving other gods. Listen to them; but warn them, and let them know what the king who will reign over them will do'

When Samuel awoke, he remembered the dream. Now he knew what he had to do, but was filled with sadness.

At his command the heads of the twelve tribes and many of the people assembled at the great rock of Ramah, the place of meeting, three days later, and standing on the rock Samuel spoke to them:

'You have asked for a king' he told them. 'But first listen to what the king who will reign over you will do. 'Some of those present glanced at each other uneasily as Samuel continued: 'He will take your sons and make them serve with his chariots and horses. Some he will assign to be commanders of thousands and commanders of fifties, and others to plough his ground and gather up his corn; still others, to make weapons of war and equipment for his chariots. Your daughters he will take into his household to act as servants He will take the best of your fields and vineyards and give them to his attendants. He will take a tenth of your grain and wine and give it to his officials, and your menservants and maidservants and the best of your cattle and horses will also become his. You yourselves will become his slaves. And when that day comes, you will cry out for relief from the king you have chosen, but the Lord your God will not answer you on that day.'

Those assembled before him fell silent. And after looking round at them Samuel demanded: 'Is this really what you really want?'

The silence continued for what seemed a long time. Then one bolder than the rest shouted:' 'Choose a king to lead us!'

At first, only a few echoed his words; then more, until finally most of the crowd took up the cry. Finally Samuel held up his hand and they fell silent once more. He looked around wearily at the sea of faces looking up at him until finally he said:

'Very well. Everyone is to go back to their homes until I summon you again.'

Some of those in front of him cheered, but others turned away half ashamed.

Chapter Two

There was a man called Kish, of the tribe of Benjamin, the smallest of the twelve tribes. He had a son called Saul, an impressive young man without equal from any tribe, standing a head taller than the rest.

One day, Kish called Saul away from feeding the cattle and told him that during the night their donkeys had trampled down the fence round their enclosure and wandered off:

'Of course, it's possible they had been stolen' Kish said grimly. 'These are troubled times. Either way, they can't have gone far, so take your servant Aram with you and bring them back. He's a skilled tracker so you should not have much difficulty. But take stout staffs both of you, just in case!'

To begin with Aram followed the donkeys trail easily enough, but after a while the tracks became increasingly difficult to pick up across the sun baked hill sides until about mid day they reached a stream. Aram examined the other side but there was no sign of the donkeys having crossed.

'Probably they have followed the stream but in which direction, it's impossible to say' he admitted.

After quenching their thirst, the two young men rested in the shade of an overhanging rock, and discussed the situation.

'You know donkeys.' Saul laughed. 'They're bound to have done what you least expect'.

You could go one way and I the other' Aram suggested.

Saul shook his head. 'No, that's no good. I think we should stay together'.

'Then let's toss for it'. Aram delved in his pouch and pulled out a small coin. 'Rough, we go up stream, smooth we go down.'

'All right'. Saul watched as his companion spun the coin in the air. Then they both leaned forward to examine where it had fallen.

'Smooth' Aram called as he picked it up. 'Come on'

He set off splashing through the water followed by Saul, but the sun was still hot and after an hour they rested again after taking a drink in the shade of a wild fig tree, having seen no sign of the animals.

After a minute or two. Saul stood up and said: 'Look, I think we should go back or my father will stop thinking about the donkeys and start worrying about us!'

Aram stood up and shaded his eyes with his hand looking into the distance, then pointed. 'There's a small town over there.'

Saul followed his gaze.

'I think that's Ramah. Where the Prophet Samuel lives'. He turned to Aram.

'They say he knows everything.'

'Could we ask him about the donkeys?'

'I don't know.' Saul laughed. 'Wouldn't he think it a cheek? He must get asked rather more important questions!

Aram returned his grin. 'Well, he can only tell us to go away. But I heard he's kind to animals . . . . and mad people!'

'That settles it then.' Saul laughed again. 'We have lost some animals and we must be mad to ask him about them!'

'We can give him this coin to give to the poor' Aram said pulling it out of his pouch again.

Saul nodded. 'Let's go then'

By the time they reached Ramah the heat had gone out of the day. At the foot of the hill on which the town stood were several wells fed by the stream which disappeared into the ground a mile away.

Some girls were there filling their pails with water before setting off to carry them home.

Seeing the two good looking strangers approaching, they stopped what they were doing and nudged each other giggling.

"Welcome!' one bolder than the rest called out as Saul and Aram drew level.' Would you like some water?

'Thank you,' Aram turned and glanced at Saul with a grin.

At this, all the young women grounded their pails with a splash and unhooked the cups each carried at their waists in the rush to be one of those from whom the strangers would choose to accept a drink.

'Thank you'. Saul took the cup offered by a handsome red headed young women who seemed a year or two older than the rest. 'What is your name?

'Esther' The girl smiled. 'And what are you doing visiting Ramah? Are you lost? In which case I can offer you a bed for the night'

'It's not fair' one of the others burst out. She's got a husband!'

Esther turned to her sharply. 'But he's away fighting the Philistines' she said, before turning back to Saul and smiling ruefully. 'Who knows if I will ever see him again!'

Aram turned to Saul after speaking to a fair haired girl and handing her cup back to her.

'We have come to see Samuel' he said pointedly.'

'Then you are in luck' another of the girls put in. 'He has only just returned from a meeting of the Tribes at the great rock outside our town.'

'There is to be a sacrifice and feast' another added eagerly. 'Hurry. As you enter the Town you may find him sitting in the gateway before he goes up to the High Place to eat. The people will not start until he comes. He must bless the sacrifice first, then those invited will eat. If you go up now, you should find him'

In fact, Samuel was resting in the shade of an old olive tree at the rear of his house from which he could see the hillside below as well as other houses and orchards to the edge of the town and the countryside beyond.

It was a favourite spot where he could sit and not be disturbed unless his servant came to tell him that someone had called on urgent business. 'Mind you' as he often reflected "most people considered whatever was troubling them 'urgent" But he had come to trust the judgement of Agag, a slave whom he had given his freedom when a grateful follower had given him to the old priest more years ago than either of them cared to remember, but had chosen to remain as his companion and helper.

Agag knew his master got easily tired these days but that he would have gone to his grave rather than turn away anyone deserving his help. But there was a limit, even for him, and the servant often sent petitioners away with some good advice of his own. After all, he had not been with Israel's leader all these years without some wisdom rubbing off on him!

Samuel knew he did this, but as his sons had proved themselves totally unworthy to follow in his footsteps and had been rejected by the people, he had felt the burden of carrying the leadership increasingly demanding. And now, he knew, he must make the biggest decision of his life.

Last night he had prayed, without an answer. But now, as he sat in the cool of the evening preparing to go where the people were expecting him, a voice he recognised immediately spoke to him

'I have sent a man to you. He is from the tribe of Benjamin. Anoint him leader over my people Israel. He will deliver them from the hand of the Philistines. Then you may rest. I have looked upon my people Their cry has reached me.'

He was awakened by Agag shaking his shoulder gently.

'Master, it is time to go to the feast, Samuel looked around and saw the sun had set. He got to his feet.

'I must have dozed off'

'Yes master' The two men smiled at each other and Agag helped him to his feet.

'I feel better for it'

Samuel entered the house and walked through the small living room and out through the door leading into the narrow street.

Agag made as if to follow him.

'Do you wish me to come with you?' The servant paused as he saw his master staring at a tall young man with another coming towards him. And instead of walking past and through the gateway leading into the town, he stopped in front of them; and Samuel knew, with absolute certainty, this was the man he had dreamt of.

'Can you tells us where is the house of the one they call the Prophet?'

The young man's companion spoke and Agag answered; 'You are speaking to him'

If Saul was disturbed by the way the old man was staring at him he gave no sign, but before he could speak Samuel pulled himself together and said: 'What is your name, my son?'

Saul inclined his head and said: 'I am Saul, son of Kish. And this is my guide Arum'

Samuel nodded briefly at Arum then turned back to Saul.

'I have been expecting you'

Saul frowned.' How can that be?

'He is a prophet!' Aram hissed.

'Go up ahead of me to the place of sacrifice' Samuel told him, 'for this evening you are to eat with me, and in the morning I will let you go, but not before I tell you everything that is in front of you.'

'The donkeys', Aram put in, and the priest turned to him.

'Do not worry, they have been found.' He looked back at Saul. 'But you, son of Kish, is it not through you that all the desire of Israel for a king will be fulfilled. You and all your father's family?'

Saul was now almost speechless, but after glancing at Aram beside him he stammered: 'But I am from the smallest tribe of Israel, and my father's tribe the smallest in the Tribe of Benjamin?' Why are you saying such a thing to me'?

Samuel smiled, and rested his hand on his shoulder.

'You will see. But now we must go. They are expecting us.

Aram and Agag watched Samuel lead Saul away from them and through the gateway out of sight.

Agag turned to the young man standing beside him.

'He has been waiting a long time.'

'Should I go with them?'

The older man shook his head.

'They will come back here'

Aram suddenly grinned. 'and so will I. But for now, I have an invitation!'

10

After the sacrifice, Samuel led Saul to the hall crowded with the elders and chief men of the town where they were to eat. As Samuel's invited guest, Saul was greeted with great honour and he was seated beside him at the head of the top table. But Samuel had warned Saul to say nothing about what he had told him earlier.

After the meal was over, he led the younger man back to his house and they sat on the roof long into the night while Samuel explained to him that it was the Lord himself who had told him in a dream who he had chosen to be King.

'You must keep the Covenant God made with our ancestors when he led them out of slavery in Egypt and settled them in this land which he had promised them,' Samuel told him gravely. 'And as long as you do, he will grant you victory over our enemies and banish for ever the threat of the nations surrounding us, particularly the Philistines.'

At daybreak Samuel called Saul who had spent the rest of the night on the roof and told him to get ready with his servant who was waiting for him so he could send them on their way.

But first, he took a small flask of oil, and after making Saul kneel down, poured it on his head and embraced him saying; 'The Lord himself has anointed you leader over his people' Then he bade Saul stand up again before continuing: 'When you leave me today you will meet two men on your way home. They will tell you that the donkeys you set out to find have been found and that now your father is worried about his son. Go on from there and when you reach the great tree of Tabor you will meet another three men on their way to the altar at Bethel. They will greet you and offer you two loaves of bread which you will accept from them. From there you will meet a company of prophets coming down from the high place with harps, tambourines and flutes singing and praising God. And the Spirit of the Lord will come upon you in power and you will join with them. And as you do, you will be changed into a different person. Once these signs are fulfilled, do whatever comes into your heart, for God is with you. But go ahead of me first to Gilgal. I will certainly come to you there and offer a sacrifice, but you must wait for me seven days until I come and tell you what you are to do.'

Chapter Three

Before Joshua led the Israelites across the Jordan to occupy the land promised to him he defeated and expelled the Amorites who occupied the territory immediately east of the river where they were due to cross and who had shown them unremitting hostility. This had not been his original intention but he judged it unwise to leave his rear unguarded and subject to attack at a time when they still had to overcome enemies of unknown strength in front of them

After the Amorites had fled, although he considered they were unlikely to present a threat in the immediate future, he allocated their territory to the tribes of Reuben, Gad and half of the tribe of Manasseh so as not to leave it open to reoccupation. This on condition that most of their fighting men should cross the Jordan and remain with their brother tribes until they too had been settled.

This they did, and eventually Joshua sent them home with his blessing to join their families in the construction of new towns and villages. But four hundred years had passed since then, and while the Israelites up to the time of Samuel had become divided and weakened, the Amorites had grown strong enough to begin regular raids into what had been their territory until finally, just after Nahash had become their king, word came that the priest who had managed to reunite the Israelite tribes had been rejected by his followers who now seemed to be leaderless.

Nahash led a formidable army and overcame what resistance they met with great savagery butchering men, women and children without pity until within a day they reached the gates of the town of Jabesh into which everyone who could had taken sanctuary. The situation seemed hopeless and it did not take long to agree to ask for terms of surrender.

The answer the delegation who brought back was worse than their worst nightmares. 'Everyone who gave themselves up would be spared, but only after having their right eye gouged out—even the children.'

They were given three days to open the gates or face complete destruction.

Some argued that this would be better. Nahash was not to be trusted. He was a brutal man who probably would do both.

So it was agreed they would not open the gates, but try to smuggle someone over the walls when it got dark to cross the Jordan and seek help. And if it was not forthcoming, they would fight to the death.

Fortunately, the Ammonites, liked nothing better, short of slitting the throats of their enemies, than to eat and drink—particularly the latter, and as the sound of their revelry started to die down round about midnight, two young men were lowered from the walls and escaped without being seen.

Samuel had sent out messengers to all the tribes summoning them to Gilgal, a sacred place where the tribes under Joshua had rested for the first time after crossing the Jordan.

They assembled early in the morning and stood before Samuel who stood on the sacred rock to speak to them.

'This is what the Lord, the God of Israel says; I brought you up out of Egypt and have delivered you from all the kingdoms that would have oppressed you. But you have rejected your God who saved you from all calamities and said, 'no, set a king over us'. So now present yourselves before the Lord by your tribes and clans'.

Agag who had been standing in the background helped him down. Then, when they had done as he had commanded, Samuel began to walk along the the assembled ranks and eventually stopped in front of the tribe of Benjamin.

This caused some surprise as Benjamin was the smallest tribe and several of the others grumbled to each other.

Ignoring this, Samuel called the various clans of Benjamin forward one after the other, rejecting all until the clan of Matri stood before him.

'Where is the family of Kish?' Samuel demanded

Kish himself stepped forward and raised his hand

'You are Kish the father of Saul?

Kish inclined his head.

'Yes sir'

Samuel looked around.

'I don't see him Where is he?

'Kish looked over his shoulder for a few moments before turning back.

'I don't know sir. He came with us.'

'He's looking after the baggage' one of Saul's brothers called out. 'He seemed very nervous!'

'He is a fine young man, but never pushes himself forward' his father admitted.

'Let him be found and brought here.'

Kish turned and nodded to the young man who had spoken who immediately ran to do the priest's bidding.

'The rest of you, remain where you are,' Samuel ordered

He returned to the base of the rock, reaching it just as Saul was led from behind the baggage wagons. The priest beckoned him forward and those who watched saw he stood a head taller than anyone else. Samuel took his hand and the two of them mounted the rock together where he turned to face the crowd below and called out in a loud voice.

'Do you see the man the Lord had chosen? There is no one like him in all Israel' He took Saul's hand and raised it above his head, whereupon most in the watching crowd began to shout 'Long live King Saul' But a few looked at each other and muttered 'How can this fellow save us?'

There was a feast to celebrate, but half way through the two young men from Jabash arrived and the mood of celebration turned to dismay as they related what had happened.

But Saul stood up raising a spear and in a loud voice shouted: Who will come with me to rescue our brothers?'

A cheer greeted this, and after Saul and those willing to go with him knelt before Samuel to receive his blessing, they set of with the two young men to guide them.

Kish looked after them with a worried expression and murmured 'They are not many to face a large Ammonite army—and with so few weapons!'

Overhearing, Samuel turned to him and said 'Do not worry about your son. The Lord will be with him'.

By the time they had waded across the river it was nearly light and Saul turned to their guides.

'We can find our own way now. Return to the city and tell your people that by the time the sun is hot the day after tomorrow they will be free'

The two looked at each other then turned back at Saul.

'But how?' one of them asked, looking round at the small number.

Saul smiled grimly.

'You will see. Trust me, and trust the Lord!'

After another moment's hesitation, the pair nodded, and moved off into the night.

When they reached the walls, one gave a signal and a rope was thrown down to them.

The people were delighted when they were told that the new King would rescue them and sent a message to the Ammonites that in two days time day they would surrender and they could do whatever they pleased with them.

Before it got light, Saul divided his small force into three, putting one third under Kish, his brother and another third under Abner his cousin, ordering these two to circle round the Ammonite camp then lie out of sight until darkness fell again, and until about mid-night, when Nahash and his men would have drunk their fill.

When news of the impending surrender was received the whole Ammonite army was relieved. Although they had overwhelming numbers, taking a city with siege ramps was a tricky business and some of them were bound to pay for it with their lives.

That night, Nahash and his commanders were in a particularly good mood and drank fulsomely as they boasted what they were going to do with their captives—particularly the women. And of course, at least six children would be burned alive as a thank offering to their god Molech.

When the moon rose Saul and his men ran silently through the enemy camp picking up the weapons which had mostly been left outside the tents, arming themselves and throwing the rest away into the darkness. Only one or two of the Ammonites saw them, but did not realise who they were until it was too late and they had been silenced.

The three groups then began to throw the remains of the fires into the tents then waited for those inside to try and escape.

The slaughter was overwhelming, and seeing what was happening from the walls, the fighting men inside the city flung open the gates and stormed out to join in the Ammonite destruction.

This continued until day break, by which time no two of the invaders were left together. Nahash was one of the few who managed to escape, but he was overtaken by Abner and his men who brought him back to Saul.

The two kings looked at each other curiously and the Ammonite thought that he was going to be spared after all. But after a moment Saul turned to his cousin and gave an order. Nahash did not understand. He did a moment later when Abner plunged a captured spear into his body.

Saul and the others returned to Samuel at Gilgal in great triumph to find those who had grumbled against him tied hand and foot.

Then the people said to Samuel: 'These are those who said Saul was not fit to reign over us. Surely they should be put to death?'

The Priest turned to Saul, but he said: 'The Lord has rescued Israel. No one shall be put to death today'

Samuel nodded in approval and raising his voice said; 'Then let us confirm King Saul before the Lord' and while all the people gathered round, Samuel anointed Saul after which there was a great celebration

Chapter four

Saul was thirty years old when he became king and he reigned over Israel for forty-two years.

Despite his initial humility, over the years, the things that the prophet Samuel had predicted when first the people came to him and demanded a king came to pass and gradually Saul began to take the privileges of Kingship for granted, becoming increasingly more autocratic. Despite this, Saul's eldest son, Jonathan, remained popular with the people and the Army, which he often led in his Father's place. He was the only one who ever stood up to his father, which usually infuriated Saul who was jealous of his position and power. But despite this, he recognised in his son a wise head and trusted him more than anyone else for advice, for Samuel had retired to his home town of Ramah.

In addition to Jonathan, Saul had two other Sons—Ishvi and Malki-Shua, but unlike their elder brother they took little interest in matters of state and were quite content to flatter their father and enjoy the privileges of being royal princes. The name of Saul's eldest daughter was Merab and his youngest Michal. The commander of Saul's army was his cousin Abner, the son of his father's brother, who had been with him from the beginning.

All the days of Saul there was bitter war with the Philistines, neither side gaining total victory, and whenever Saul saw a mighty or brave man, he took him into his service.

Although he never saw Saul again, word came to Samuel of Saul's increasingly tyrannical behaviour which caused him great distress. Then, one night, in a vision, he heard God speak to him.

'How long will you grieve that you anointed Saul King, for I have rejected him as king over Israel.'

Samuel tossed restlessly on his bed. 'Surely it could only be a dream?' But then he heard again that voice which had first spoken to him as a very young assistant to Eli the Priest over seventy years ago, and this time there could be no mistake

'Fill your horn with oil and be on your way. I am sending you to Jesse of Bethlehem. I have chosen one of his sons to be king in Saul's place'

The old man trembled. 'How can I go?' he pleaded. 'Saul will hear about it and kill me!'

But the Lord said: 'Take a heifer with you and say I have come to sacrifice to the Lord. Invite Jesse to the sacrifice, and I will show you what to do. You are to anoint the one I indicate'

Some of the sheep had paused to listen to the young shepherd, and when he finally stopped playing and lowered the pipes smiling they turned away and resumed grazing on the lush grass and herbs which covered the hills close to Bethlehem before the summer sun burned everything brown. But by then, his father Jesse and his brothers would have made hay in the fields surrounding their farm and brought it into the barns, sufficient to see them through until the rains came and the first green shoots appeared on the hills again promising the renewal of life upon which the family depended.

The rains rarely failed, or arrived too late to allow the grass as well as other crops to become established before the summer heat made further growth impossible. Not in the life time of Jesse or his fathers before him going back several generations, but it <u>had</u> happened. Then there was famine throughout the whole country and people said it was because the Lord was angry because Israel had broken the covenant by worshiping the gods of the surrounding nations, with their 'detestable practices'; so they were careful to follow the rules laid down by Moses and anyone found guilty of disobeying these was punished severely. But some thought secretly that their enemies the Philistines did not follow the Law, yet they seemed to enjoy the same abundant harvests These opinions they kept to themselves.

Such thoughts were far from the mind of David, Jesses son as he got to his feet and started to walk a little way along the ridge to some fresh pasture and all the flock followed him without question with the big ram, Hamma in the lead at David's heel.

They came to a small group of old olive trees which had been left to themselves many years ago, and here David sat under the shade of one of them, his back to the trunk and pulled out the pipes from his pouch again. He raised them to his lips, but then hesitated and frowned slightly. He was barely seventeen years old and normally had little to trouble him. But news had come from Gibeah, the King's city, by a traveller the previous evening that the Philistines had been seen by one of Israelite outposts massing a great army just a few miles from the border, and that could only mean that very soon his brothers who were of military age would be called to their units in the King's army.

Despite his age, David had been taught well by his elder brother Eliab who was an officer commanding a hundred men and was a match with both spear and sword with any of his other brothers, but he was not permitted to go with them, not only because of his youth but because his father would need him more than ever to help him with the work.

David's brow furrowed as he thought about this, but suddenly he heard the bleat of a sheep in distress and jumped to his feet to see the flock scattering over the hillside as two leopards made off, each with a lamb between their teeth.

Despite his ability with the sword, he was rarely allowed to carry one as they were kept for when the brothers went to war, but he was even more skilled with the sling he always carried and could drop any eagle threatening the flock even as it swooped to attack.

Drawing it now he managed to catch one of the animals in the ribs with a stone causing it to drop the lamb before making off, but the other was out of range before he could cast again leaving him with no choice but to grab the wooden staff he used to keep the sheep together and set off in pursuit.

He eventfully caught up with the thief at the bottom of the slope where there was a small stream and gave it a whack with the staff causing it to drop it's prey. But instead of running off like the other animal, it turned and sprang at him.

David managed to dodge its lunge and so began a series of attacks by the leopard, with David just managing to keep out of reach, while striking the animal round the head until finally it gave up, and with a final snarl, turned and loped off after its companion.

David picked up the lamb and found it to be relatively unharmed, but when he got back to where the other lay he found its neck had been broken and it was dead.

After rounding up the others, he set off for home carrying the dead lamb. It was not impossible the big cats would try again.

He approached the town with a heavy heart knowing his brothers would mock him for not having saved both lambs and that his father would probably make him pay for the dead one.

When Samuel arrived in Bethlehem, the elders of the Town trembled that such a great prophet should visit them. 'Do you come in peace? the chief elder asked apprehensively,

'Yes, in peace.' Samuel smiled, then he turned and nodded to his servant Agag who in turn handed over the rope by which he had been leading a young heifer.

'Take this animal and prepare it' Samuel continued. 'I have come to sacrifice to the Lord. Consecrate yourselves, and when all is ready come to the sacrifice with me'. (In those days, an animal offered for sacrifice was only partially burned on the altar and the rest was distributed as 'fellowship offerings' among those who had come to the ceremony).

'In the mean time, I wish to visit the family of Jesse. Will someone show me the way?'

'Of course, my lord,' the elder said eagerly. 'My son here will take you'

He turned and nodded at a young man watching, who immediately stepped forward.

When they reached the farm, Samuel dismissed his young guide with a word of thanks and turned to face Jesse who had hurried out of the house followed by his whole family and allowed himself to be conducted to the rear of the house where they were able to sit in the shade while the women hurried indoors to fetch water and sweetmeats.

He then swore Jesse and his sons on solemn oath not to reveal what they were about to witness. 'Until such time as The Lord himself will reveal to you'

Then Samuel rose to his feet and brought out a small flask of oil.

23

'Tell your sons to stand together on the far side of the court yard, then call them forward one at a time in order of seniority.'

Jesse, who had also risen to his feet gestured to his sons who did as they were bidden then stood waiting. If it had occurred to any of them to ask what it was all about, they thought better of it

'Begin with the eldest' Samuel prompted.

Jesse nodded and called out: 'Eliab'

The eldest brother approached, and as he did so Samuel saw that he was tall and strong looking and thought to himself 'Surely this is the one the Lord has chosen?'

But as the young man stood in front of them, a voice inside his head warned: 'Do not consider his appearance or his height. I do not look at the things a man looks at but at his heart. He is not the one I have chosen'

So Samuel turned to Jesse and shook his head. 'Let the next eldest step forward.' he said, So Jesse turned to Eliab and indicated he should go back to where the others were standing before calling out: 'Abinadab'. So the second son came and stood before them. But again, after a moment the prophet shook his head and Shammah, the next in age came to stand in his place, and after him, the four remaining sons.

When the last had returned to his place, Samuel said: 'The Lord has not chosen any of these. Are these all the sons you have? But before Jesse could answer Eliab looked over their shoulders and called out.' There's David. Late as usual!'

Samuel turned and said: 'Come here my son'

'This is my youngest son. He has been tending the sheep' Jesse told him.

David came forward intending to confess the loss of the lamb. But before he could say anything Samuel saw that he was not as tall as his brothers but good-looking and of strong appearance, and the Lord said to him. 'He is the one. Anoint him'. He ordered David to kneel. 'For the Lord has chosen you before all others to lead his people and to deliver him from the hands of their enemies'

Scarcely knowing what he was doing, David knelt wide eyed in front of him as the others crowded nearer and Samuel anointed him with the oil.

Then the priest reminded them all of their oath and they went up together to the sacrifice and feast. After this, Samuel went back to Ramah.

But from then on, the Spirit of God came on David in power.

Chapter five

A t first light, a young girl in the village of Socoh in the territory of Judah who had gone out to milk the family goat so they could have milk for breakfast happened to glance across to the ridge of hills to the south-west which were just catching the first rays of the sun behind her and saw something which caused her to drop her bucket and go running indoors to fetch her parents who soon came running out, her Mother carrying the child she had been in the middle of feeding, to look in the direction their daughter was pointing.

The distant ridge was now easier to see and for a few seconds they gazed at what appeared to be a dark wave which had already started to move down the facing slope and kept pouring over the hill, seemingly without end. Every now and then there were flashes of reflected sunlight from the front of the wave.

The man turned to his wife and said grimly: 'The Philistines. We must leave at once. Saddle two of the donkeys and get the children ready. I will go and warn our neighbours.

Long before the advance party of the Philistine army arrived, the village was deserted and one of the younger men had ridden away on one of the few horses the village possessed to ride to Gibeah to warn the king.

Saul had been expecting this invasion and arrangements were already in place to summons the reservists to join up with the regular army under Abner, who set out at once to hold the Philistine advance until these arrived and the invaders could be driven back.

But as it happened, the Philistine commander had other ideas and had already taken up a position on a hill just beyond Socoh to await Saul's army.

By the time Saul, who had waited to marshal the reservists had caught up with his cousin, he found him encamped on a hill directly opposite the Philistines with a narrow valley and a small stream between them and it was not long before it became clear why conflict between the two army's had not already been joined, as a giant of a man emerged from the Philistine ranks and marched halfway down the slope towards them.

He was over nine feet tall and had a bronze helmet on his head. His body was encased in bronze armour that weighed over a hundred and twenty-five pounds and he had a bronze javelin slung across his back. His spear shaft was like a small tree and the iron point must have weighed more than fifteen pounds. His shield bearer went ahead of him.

'Why do you huddle like cowards on top of your hill?' he shouted at the watching Israelites. 'Am I not Goliath, a Philistine and are you not servants of Saul? Choose a man and have him come down to me. If he is able to kill me, we will become your subjects; but if I overcome him you will become our subjects and serve us. This day I defy the ranks of Israel. Give me a man and let us fight each other!'

This went on for several days filling Saul and the army with dismay for none were brave enough to face the giant, and every day his taunts grew worse and the morale of the Israelites started to crumble.

Early one morning, Jesse called David and told him to take some bread and cheese to the commander of the unit in which his brothers were serving and bring back some word of assurance that they were unharmed. So, leaving the flocks in the safety of a fold with a young lad from another family to keep an eye on them, he loaded a mule and set out as Jesse had directed.

He reached the camp just as the army was going out to its battle positions and the Philistines were drawing up their lines again facing them across the valley. David left the mule with the keeper of supplies and ran to the battle lines to greet his brothers.

As he was talking with them Goliath stepped out from his lines and shouted his usual insults, while those in the front row of the Israelites looked at each other with fear. To an outside observer it would have been obvious that the Philistine plan was to so demoralise their opponents, they would admit defeat without the need for a battle

Some of the Israelites close to where David's brothers were standing said to each other: 'Do you see how this man keeps coming out to defy us? The King will give great wealth to the man who kills him. He will also give him his daughter in marriage and exempt his father's family from any taxes or tributes!'

David turned to them and said: 'Who is this dog that he should defy the armies of the living God?'

But when Eliab heard him he was annoyed and demanded; 'Why have you come here? Have you left the flocks out in the desert?'

'I know how conceited he is' his brother Shammah added 'He's only come to watch the battle and see us all get killed!'

But David ignored them and shouted across to another group close by asking the same thing.

The King's tent was not far away, and overhearing the argument, Saul sent for him, and when brought before him David said: 'My Lord, let no one lose heart on account of this Philistine. Your servant will go and fight him'

Despite his deep concern, the king had to suppress a smile as he glanced for a moment at Abner beside him before turning back and saying gently 'You are not able to fight him, my son. You are only a boy. He has been a fighting man from his youth'

David coloured, but he answered vehemently: 'Your servant has been keeping his father's sheep. Often a leopard, a lion or a bear tries to carry off one of the sheep but I go after them and strike them so they let them go. I have killed both a lion and a bear and this uncircumcised Philistine will be like one of them because he has defied the armies of the living God. The Lord, who delivered me from the paw of the lion and the bear will deliver me from the hand of this Philistine!'

Saul hesitated and glanced again at Abner before saying quietly 'Perhaps the boy is right. Perhaps the Lord will save him? There is certainly no one else willing'.

Abner shook his head, but after a second's hesitation Saul called over his shoulder and ordered his attendants to bring his own armour and sword.

David put them on, after which, he tried to walk around. But Saul was half a head taller and he turned to the king and said: 'I cannot go in this armour my Lord. I am not used to it, and this sword is too heavy for me'. So he took it off, and taking his staff in his hand set off down the hill towards the Philistine, watched by both armies who fell silent when they saw what was happening—except his brother Eliab, who muttered; 'Father will kill us when he hears about this!'

David paused when he reached the stream to select five smooth stones which he put in the shepherd's bag tied to his waist

Meanwhile, Goliath, with his shield bearer kept coming closer. Then the giant stopped and looked more closely at David. And seeing he was only a boy, he despised him.

'Am I a dog that you come at me with sticks' he snarled? 'Come here and I'll give your flesh to the vultures!'

But David stood his ground unflinching.

'You come at me with sword and spear,' he shouted back. 'But I come against you in the name of the Lord Almighty, the God of the armies of Israel, whom you have defied. This day the Lord will hand you over to me and I'll strike you down and cut off your head. Then we will give the carcasses of your army to the vultures and the whole earth will know there is a God in Israel'

With a shout of rage, Goliath drew his sword, and pushing the armour bearer to one side rushed at David.

Those watching with Saul from the top of the hill held their breath. But David quickly reached into his bag, and taking out a stone, he pulled his sling from his belt almost in one movement and slung the stone so it struck the charging Philistine in the centre of his forehead.

Goliath stumbled with a look of surprise on his face, then pitched face forward onto the ground

David ran towards him and the servant turned tail and ran. When he reached where Goliath was lying, he took the giant's sword from his hand and with one blow, cut off his head.

A huge cheer went up from the Israelite army, and led by Abner, they charged down the hill towards the enemy lines. But when the Philistines saw that their champion was dead they turned and ran. And with a great shout the men of Israel surged after them so the enemy dead were strewn along the road all the way back to their cities of Gath and Ekron.

David climbed back up the hill carrying Goliath's sword in one hand and his severed head in the other to where Saul and his son Jonathan stood waiting to congratulate him.

'Who's Son are you?' Saul asked as he was slapping David on the back with the others.

When David told him, Saul promised that he would keep his promise. Jesse and his family would be honoured throughout the land and would pay no further taxes.

'As for you,' Saul continued, 'If you are willing, I would have you in my service. 'Though you are young, I see you are a formidable warrior, and I would have such close to me in times of danger!'

David willingly agreed. Then Saul turned to his son.

'This is my son Jonathan,' Saul told him; then to Jonathan he said: 'I want you to take personal responsibility for this young man's training, and promotion to a command as soon as possible.'

Jonathan nodded, and the two young men grinned at each other and clasped hands.

And so began a friendship that would last a lifetime. But as the people came out rejoicing to meet Saul as he returned home in triumph with tambourines and lutes, singing and dancing, the women sang: 'Saul has slain his thousands and David his tens of thousands'

This did not please Saul, and he turned to Abner in the chariot beside him and grumbled: 'They have credited that young man with tens of thousands, but me with only thousands. What more can he get but the kingdom?'

Abner tried to make light of it, but he knew that look, and from then on Saul kept a jealous eye on David.

Chapter six

Over the following months, Jonathan taught David everything he knew of the military arts and David joined him in patrolling the borders of Saul's kingdom, pursuing raiders when necessary to recover spoils and live stock and occasionally making raids themselves to teach aggressive neighbouring tribes a lesson. Despite his youth, It was not long before David had acquired skills with the sword that had been especially made for him far beyond those he had been taught by his eldest brother, and with bow and javelin the equal of Jonathan himself.

The two of them grew ever closer, and one day Jonathan took off his royal robe and put it on David. He promoted him to a high position in the army and they swore a covenant of friendship. The men Jonathan put David in charge of loved and trusted him. Sometimes in the evening they would ask him to play for them and he would get out a harp and sing songs which he had made up himself, praising God and the wonder of his creation. His reputation as a musician as well as a warrior soon spread throughout Israel.

Jonathan often spoke favourably to his father about David, but Saul's response was negative, more often than not, and he realised the King still harboured jealousy towards his friend.

In addition to which, Saul often had fits of depression which lasted for days.

Seeing an opportunity, not only to help his father, but David at the same time, Jonathan suggested that the King should invite David to play for him when he felt particularly low, and after some persuasion, Saul agreed.

Everyone close to the King was delighted that when David played and sang for him, his black moods seem to pass for a while and he became himself again, but it seemed the spirit of the Lord had left him and it was not long before David was summoned again to play. But at least, Jonathan thought, his father's attitude to his friend had changed.

For a while after the death of Goliath, the Philistines remained in their cities, but they were a people who lived for war and it was not long before they began again to probe the Israelite outposts to see which were less well defended, pointing perhaps to an opportunity for another invasion.

So Abner called all his senior officers to him, including David and planned a series of raids of their own against the Philistine outposts which, increasing of late, had intruded systematically further into Israelite territory. The officers subsequently led their men on their allotted assignments, but with mixed success. David alone, with his men, never failed to return triumphant, and Jonathan reminded his father of his promise to give Merab, his eldest sister to whoever slew Goliath. But Saul had other plans. and gave her instead to another of his officers. Then he called David into his presence and told him that he had another chance to become his son-in-law.

Michal, Jonathan's youngest sister, was in love with David and that pleased Saul for he thought to himself, she will be a snare for him. He told David that he would give Michal to him on completion of a mission deep into Philistine territory and David was so smitten with Michel that he did not realise the task he had been given would almost certainly lead to his death.

Jonathan saw at once, when he learned of the plan, what was behind it, and that his father's jealousy and fear of David was as strong as ever. He tried to dissuade his friend, without actually saying as much, and when David would not listen, planned to go with him with his own men. But Saul heard of it and ordered Jonathan to remain at Court. So early one morning David set out with his two hundred men and orders to penetrate the Philistine defences and lay waste the nearest town. To everyone's amazement they did just that and returned to a rapturous welcome.

Saul had no alternative but to keep his promise, and within two month's David and Michel were married amidst great rejoicing by the people.

It was all too much for Saul, and when David next played for him, he suddenly picked up a spear and threw it at him, but narrowly missed, giving David time to escape.

When he heard about it, Jonathan realised his father had become unbalanced and that if he were to speak to him it would have to be gently.

Picking his moment he said to his father; 'Let not the king do wrong to his servant David. He has not wronged you, and what he has done has benefited you greatly. He took his life in his hands when he slew the Philistine giant. The Lord won a great victory for Israel that day. You saw it and were glad. And since that day he has gone out and fought many battles on your behalf and has succeeded in everything you asked because the Lord is with him. Why then would you try to kill a loyal and innocent man?'

Saul was silent for a long time. Then he looked at his son and said gruffly: 'As surely as the Lord lives, David will not be put to death'.

Jonathan reported the whole conversation to David, and for a while he was with Saul as before.

War broke out again. The Philistines invaded to revenge themselves and for a while the Israelite defences buckled. Then Abner sent out David with a strong force and he struck the invaders with such ferocity the Philistines fled before him. And once again, the people turned out to welcome him home with adulation.

But as Jonathan feared, this reawakened his father's jealousy, and when he was next sitting in his house listening to David with a spear in his hand he suddenly stood up and threw it at David, again narrowly missing him.

That night, Jonathan sent a servant to David's house to warn him that his father had become so deranged he was going to send men to wait outside his house and kill him when he came out in the morning.

Michal his wife implored him leave at once and hide somewhere 'If you don't want to die' she said tearfully.

'Of course I don't want to die' David said. 'But what about you? If he is as bad as your brother says, you may be killed as well. You must come with me'

But Michal shook her head 'No. I have always been his favourite. He'll be angry but he would never harm me, I know. And I would slow you down, then we'd both get caught and then things might be different.

David hesitated, but finally he nodded, and after they had embraced, Michal let him down from a rear window with a rope in case anyone was already watching by the front door. She saw him disappear into the darkness. Then she rolled some blankets and put them into the bed to make it look as if someone was sleeping there before sitting in a chair to wait for morning.

She dozed fitfully, dreaming of she and David holding each other. But when she awoke in the morning it was with an ache in the pit of her stomach wondering if she would ever see him again.

Michal did not have long to wait before there was a knock on the door and when the servant opened it, she found an officer of the king's guard with some soldiers waiting.

'We have orders to take my lord David to the king' he told her.

The woman bowed briefly then went to the foot of the stairs and called up: 'My lady, there are men here who wish to see the master'

Michal came to the head of the stairs.

'Tell them my lord is resting'

"They say the king wants him to come at once. my lady'

Michal hesitated, then she said: 'Tell them my husband is ill and cannot be disturbed.

The woman bobbed a curtsy then went back to the door and reported what she had been told.

On receiving this message Saul was furious and sent them back saying: 'Bring him to me on his bed so that I can kill him' So they returned, and after bursting into the house forced their way upstairs and soon found the attempted deception

Mical decided to grasp the nettle of her father's anger and accompanied the soldiers back to the palace.

'Why did you deceive me and let my enemy escape?' he shouted at her.

'Because he threatened to kill me,' She shouted back. 'What would you have had me do? I hate him. It was you who made me marry him!'

Saul looked at his daughter, who then flung herself into his arms weeping. And before he knew what he was doing, he found himself comforting her.

David fled to Samuel at his home in Ramah and reported everything that had happened. Samuel advised David to remain with him for a while and not to attempt to rejoin his men. But Saul learned where David was and sent a detachment of soldiers to take him captive. But the Lord warned Samuel that the troop was on its way and he hid David.

When the Soldiers arrived they found Samuel surrounded by a band of other prophets singing praises to the Lord, whose Spirit descended on them too so that they joined in the worship and eventually returned empty handed.

Saul was furious and having had the troop commander put to death, set out himself with his personal body guard. But once more the Lord warned Samuel and when the King arrived, David was not to be seen; only Samuel surrounded by the prophets singing praises to the Lord. Then the Spirit of the Lord descended on Saul as well and he returned empty handed, baffled as to what had happened.

When Jonathan knew it was safe, he met David in secret.

'What have I done?' his friend demanded immediately. 'What is my crime? How have I wronged your father that he is trying to take my life?'

'Never', Jonathan replied. 'You are not going to die!' He paused for a moment, then went on: 'Look, my father does nothing, great or small without confiding in me. Why should he hide this if it really was his intention?'

'He has already thrown his spear at me twice and pursued me all the way to Ramah!'

Jonathan nodded. 'I know. But he is a skilled spearman. If he had really intended to kill you he would not have missed. You know how much he values you really. With all the cares of the Kingship he sometimes lashes out at anything. He has been much calmer since he met with Samuel'

David looked doubtful, but he said: 'What do you advise me to do, then? Your father knows we are friends. Perhaps he has said to himself; 'Jonathan must not know of this. Surely, as the Lord lives, and as you live, there is only a step between me and death!'

Jonathan said: 'Whatever you want me to do, I will do it.'

David thought for a moment, then he said: 'Look, tomorrow is the New Moon festival. Before, I have always dined with the king, so If, despite everything, your father remarks on my absence say to him, 'David earnestly asked my permission to go to Bethlehem, his home town because an annual sacrifice is being made for his whole clan'. If he takes the news calmly, then perhaps I am safe. But if he loses his temper, you can be sure he is determined to harm me.'

Jonathan nodded. But before he could say anything, David looked him straight in the face and said: 'As for you, show kindness to me. You and I swore eternal friendship before the Lord. If I am guilty then kill me yourself. Why leave it to your father?'

'Never' Jonathan protested. 'If I have the least inkling that my father is still determined to harm you, I swear I will warn you'.

David paused, then he said: 'How will I know if your father answers you harshly?'

Jonathan thought for a moment, then he said: 'Come; let us go to the field near the banqueting hall'

On the way, Jonathan told David that if the answer was against him, he would have to be very careful because the King would guess that his son would try and warn his friend and set someone to spy on him. David agreed.

It was dusk when they reached the field. Jonathan stopped looking around. Then he said: 'Tonight I will sound out my father and let you know. If it is unfavourable, I will send you away in safety.' He turned and pointed at a group of trees. 'Hide there early tomorrow morning. I will come out with a boy and pretend to practice with a bow. You see that rock in the middle of the field?' David nodded, and Jonathan went on: 'I will shoot three arrows to the side of it as if I were shooting at a target. Then I will send the boy to collect the arrows. If I call out to him,' look . . . . the arrows are on this side of you', then come out, for as sure as the Lord lives you are safe; there is no danger. But if I shout to him,' the arrows are beyond you,' then you must go at once, because the Lord has sent you.'

David agreed, then Jonathan said: 'May the Lord be with you as he has been with my father. And do not forget the covenant of friendship we have sworn before the Lord. Show your unfailing kindness to me and my descendents as long as we live, for it has been revealed to me that the Lord will cut off all your enemies and you will be king in my father's place. Perhaps, when that time comes, if it is the Lord's will, I may be second only to you in your kingdom.'

They embraced, then Jonathan turned and walked away into the gathering darkness, with David looking after him.

That night, when the King sat down to eat he took his usual place with his back to the wall opposite Jonathan and with Abner beside him

Next to Jonathan was a vacant place, and after eying it for a while Saul demanded to know why David's place was empty.

But when Jonathan began to explain that David had asked permission to go to a family feast in Bethlehem, Saul's anger flared up.

'You son of a perverse and rebellious woman!' he shouted. 'Don't I know you have sided with the son of Jesse to your own shame and the shame of the mother who bore you? Don't you realise that the people are already speaking of David as King and that as long as he lives on this earth, neither you or your kingdom will be established? Now bring him to me for he must die!'

The assembled company had fallen silent, but Jonathan answered defiently: 'Why should he be put to death? What has he done?

Saul stood and reached behind him for his spear that was leaning against the wall and would have cast it at his son, but Abner reached up and restrained him while Jonathan got up from the table in a fury and walked out.

Early the following morning, in peaceful contrast to the events of the night before, Jonathan entered the field carrying a bow accompanied by a young boy carrying some arrows. Unseen by either of them, but not unexpected, one of Saul's body guards slipped out of the palace and followed them at a distance.

Jonathan duly took up a position and pretended to aim at the rock in the centre of the field but in fact sent the arrows to one side. Then he sent the boy to get them, and when he was some distance shouted: 'The arrows are beyond you. Hurry, go quickly, don't stop!'

When the boy returned, Jonathan turned and walked back the way he had come, with the boy trotting at his heels looking puzzled.

'Are you not going to shoot again, Master?' he asked. But Jonathan shook his head and they disappeared into the distance, until their voices were inaudible.

The soldier who had been spying on all this emerged from his cover and looked round frowning, then he too turned on his heel with a shrug and followed them.

When he had gone, David came out from where he had been hiding. He made his way a few hundred yards in the opposite direction to a clearing where there was a horse tethered to a tree. He mounted it, then rode away.

Chapter seven

When Saul discovered that David had slipped from his grasp he instituted a nationwide search. But David, who realised that apart from Jonathan and his immediate family, who were bound to be closely watched, there was no one he could trust and decided to leave Saul's Kingdom altogether until he gave up looking for him.

He decided to make for Gath, one of the Philistine Cities where he might be able to pass himself off as a mercenary and offer his services to Maoch its king. And for this story to be plausible, he had to have some kind of weapon. But having fled in such haste he had little more than his horse and the clothes he stood up in.

Then he remembered that not far out of his way was the town of Nob where Ahimelech the priest lived who was a friend and admirer of David and to whom David had entrusted the sword of Goliath for safe keeping. It had been too heavy for him when, as a youth, he had killed the giant, but now it would do admirably.

The priest welcomed him but looked round with a puzzled expression. 'Why are you alone?' he asked as his visitor dismounted. 'Why is no one with you?'

'The King has charged me with a personal matter' David told him. 'No one is to know anything about it.' He handed the bridle of the horse to one of the priest's servants who led it away to give it water. 'My men, are going to meet me in a few hours time. We left separately, and I rode out casually and unarmed so as not to arouse anyone's curiosity, which is why I am here. I need the sword of Goliath I put in your safe keeping. It has remained for just such a moment as this.'

Shortly afterwards, both horse and rider duly refreshed, David set off again with the sword now strapped to his side and his saddle bag full of bread which the priest had given him for the journey.

But as Ahimelech was saying good bye to David he was seen by Doeg, Saul's chief shepherd, who happened to be visiting his family nearby and who immediately recognised him. And although he did not feel more than idle curiosity at the time, it was to rebound on the priest's head later with terrible consequences.

Oblivious of how he had unwittingly put his friend's life in danger, David rode on and eventually reached his destination At first he was welcomed by the King of Gath, but it was not long before he was recognised. And although Maoch accepted, after David had explained how Saul had turned against him, that he was no longer a threat; besides which, the rules of hospitality forbade any harm being done to one under his protection, David became increasingly uneasy as there were plenty of inhabitants of the City with relatives who had died at his hand and who would not have the same reservations about seeking revenge. He decided to move on, and early one morning without telling anyone rode to the desert oasis of Adullam.

Here. he found a number of other fugitive outlaws sheltering from Saul's wrath for various reasons in a large cave. These welcomed him, and when told of what had happened immediately pledged allegiance to him and were soon turned from a leaderless rabble into a small but competent band of fighting men.

One of his first acts was to send some of his followers to fetch his family telling them to put the live stock in the care of friends and leave at once as surely it would not be long before Saul decided to vent his anger on them.

Others joined him: those who were in distress or in debt, or could not pay their taxes and their farms had been seized by the king's bailiffs, until there were four hundred fighting men at his command.

But David realised that the kind of life he was likely to have to lead would be too much for his mother and father, and when they were rested, he set out with a few of his followers and took them to the king of Moab, who was no friend of Saul and who readily agreed to care for them until, as David put it, 'he learned what God would do for him.'

Shortly after returning to Adullam, the prophet Gad arrived and said to David:

'The Lord says 'do not stay here but go back to the land of Judah, the land of your forefathers', so David and his men left and went into the forest of Hereth.

News of this eventually reached Saul. And when he next sat under the tamarisk tree on the hill of Gibeah with his spear in his hand and all his officials gathered around him he said to them: 'Listen to me, would David, the son of Jesse have given all of you fields and vineyards? Would he have made you commanders of thousands and given you important positions?'

Those around him looked uneasily at each other as Saul continued more harshly: 'No one tells me when my son makes a covenant with the son of Jesse! None of you is concerned about me or tells me that Jonathan has incited my so called servant to lie in wait for me as he does today!'

Then Doeg, who was standing with the other officials said: 'I saw David come to Ahimelech the priest at Nob. The priest gave him provisions and the sword of Goliath. I did not attach any importance to it at the time but now . . . . I am sorry, my Lord, I should have spoken before.' He waited for Saul's anger to break over him, but the King's mind was already racing ahead.

Saul sent for Ahimelech and his whole family who were also priests at Nob. They assembled before the King, who said to them: 'Why have you conspired against me giving the son of Jesse bread and a sword so that he rebelled against me and lies in wait for me as he does today?' But Ahimelech protested:

'My lord, who, of all your servants is as loyal as David, the King's son in law, captain of your body guard and highly respected in your household? Was that day the first time he came to me or asked me to enquire of God for him? Let not the king accuse your servant or any of my family, for I knew nothing about this whole affair. Lord David told me he was on a personal mission on your behalf, so naturally, I did not enquire into the King's business'.

But Saul snarled: 'You shall surely die, Ahimelech, you and your whole family'. He turned to the guards standing by his side.

'Kill them all. He is lying to save his own skin. They knew he was fleeing from me, yet did not tell me, and if it had not been for this man,' pointing at Doeg, 'I would not have known. They deserve to die . . . all of them. Cut off their heads, or must I do it myself!'

But the guards shrank back; 'My Lord, they are Levites, chosen to serve at the Lord's altar' one stammered.

They are guilty of treason!'

But still none dared to draw his sword, and after a moment Saul rose to his feet and drew his own sword and handed it to Doeg.

'Here, you. Strike them down and I might not remember your forgetfulness as I should.!'

The chief shepherd took the sword and for a few seconds stood with it hanging down and his head bowed. Then he took a deep breath, and swinging round to face Ahimelech, decapitated the priest with a single blow sending his head rolling to Saul's feet.

Even the King seemed shocked at this, as if some remaining shred of sanity recognised the enormity of what had just happened, but he watched unprotesting as Doeg walked along the ranks of the other priests and killed them one by one; some cleanly, some requiring more than one blow, but none resisted and eventually the ground in front of Saul was covered in blood and dead bodies.

Only one escaped; Abiathar, son of Ahimelech who had been standing at the back. He turned and fled unseen by Saul, and if anyone else witnessed, they remained silent. After several days he reached David and told him what had happened. David was immediately filled with remorse.

'I am responsible for the death of your whole father's family,' he confessed. 'But stay with me and don't be afraid. The man who may seek your life is seeking mine also. You will be safe with me'.

Shortly after this, news reached David that the Philistines were besieging the Judean town of Keilah and looting the surrounding countryside.

Despite having to run for his life, Abithar, who was also a priest, had snatched the sacred ephod from his father's house before escaping and had brought it with him. This was the priestly garment which by tradition the chief priest put on when seeking the word of the Lord, so David asked him to put it on and enquire if he should go and attack the Philistines.

And through Abithar the Lord answered: 'Go . . . attack the Philistines and save Keilah'

But David's men protested: 'Hidden in the forest we are afraid. How much more then if we go against the Philistines!'

So David enquired again and once more the Lord said: 'Go down to Keilah. I am going to give the Philistines into your hand'.

So David persuaded them and they went together to Keilah and fought the Philistines, inflicting heavy losses on them and saved the people of the town.

This was the first time David enquired of the Lord but from then on no one doubted when he did so in future

Saul was told that David had gone to Keilah, and smiled grimly. 'God has handed him over to me' he announced. 'David has entered a trap by entering a town with gates and bars'. He summonsed all his forces to go down to Keilah to besiege it. But David heard he was on his way and asked Abithar to inquire if the citizens of Keilah would hand him over to Saul to save the town and their own lives. And when the Lord confirmed that that was just what would happen, David and his men, about six hundred in all, left the town and kept moving from place to place.

When Saul was told they had escaped from Keilah, he did not go there.

David stayed in the desert strongholds and in the hills of the desert of Ziph. Day after day Saul searched for him but God did not give David into his hands.

Samuel died and all Israel assembled and mourned for him. They buried him at his home in Ramah then David moved on into the desert of Maon.

Here there was a man who had property at Carmel and was very wealthy. He had a thousand goats and three thousand sheep which roamed the desert, as well as fertile land which yielded rich harvests. His name was Nabul.

His wife's name was Abigail. She was an intelligent and beautiful women, but her husband was surly and mean in his dealings. David did not know this.

On more than one occasion rustlers would have raided Nabal's flocks which were too extensive to guard closely, even with the number of shepherds in his employment, but after David's men had seen them off on three occasions the would be thieves gave up.

But they lived hand to mouth, and when David heard that Nabul was celebrating another abundant harvest and shearing, which he owed in no small measure to the protection which David and his men had provided, David sent some of his men to Nabul to congratulate him on his good fortune at this festive time and remind him of the help they had given him in the expectation that he would be inclined to share with them some of the riches he now enjoyed.

They found Nabul celebrating with his friends and already drunk. And far from showing his gratitude, he insulted them.

'Who is this David?' he scoffed, turning to wave airily at his friends, who grinned dutifully.

'Who is this son of Jesse?' he demanded turning back to snarl at his visitors?. 'Many servants are breaking away from their masters these days. Why should I take the bread, meat and wine I have saved for my shearers and give it to men coming from who knows where? Get rid of them!'

He waved at his servants then turned his back to raise his goblet for another toast to his cronies, who sniggered again dutifully. So David's men were forced to return empty handed.

But not everyone who witnessed this humiliation laughed.

Nabul's chief steward went urgently to Abigail who had slipped away unnoticed from the drunken festivities before David's men arrived and told her what had happened.

'These men were very good to us', he said urgently. 'Night and day they were a wall around us all the time we were herding the sheep so nothing was missing.'

Abigail looked at him anxiously. 'What do you want me to do?' she said.

'Anything to make up for the insult. Disaster is hanging over our master and all of us. David is an honest man but there is no one like him when aroused to anger and he is not likely to let this insult pass Our master is too drunk to realise what he has done'

Abigail nodded. 'He never listens to anyone even when he's sober!' she said. 'But quickly. There is no time to lose!'

Leaving her husband and his friends to their drunken revelries, Abigail and the chief steward assembled a string of camels loaded with all kinds of provisions and set off to meet David. The steward protested that the mission was fraught with danger. There was no way of telling what kind of mood David would be in by now and his mistress should remain in the comparative safety of the camp. But Abigail insisted that David had never been known to harm women so perhaps they would be safer if she accompanied them. (Secretly, she was also intrigued to meet this David of whom it was said even the king was afraid)

They came to a ravine and as they began their decent, there was David and his men descending from the other side.

David had just said to Abithar who was riding beside him: 'It's been useless—all our watching over this Nabul's property in the desert so that nothing was missing. May God witness if by morning I leave alive one male of all who belong to him.'

With the approach of night the two groups did not see each other until they met at the foot of the ravine, and while David and those with him drew their swords, Abigail slipped from her mount and prostrated herself at David's feet.

'My Lord, let the blame be on me alone. Please let your servant speak to you.'

David too dismounted and, sheathing his sword, reached out his hand and lifted Abigail to her feet.'

'Who are you?' he said when he had recovered from his surprise. Not only was a woman the last person he had expected to meet out in the desert after dark, but one whose beauty astonished him.

Abigail lowered her eyes for a moment then looked up to meet his gaze and said: 'I am Abigail, wife of that drunken fool Nabal. I beg you pay no more attention to him and believe me when I say I did not see the men you sent to him. He is both greedy and wicked and no more worthy of your attention than a gnat!'

David grinned suddenly. 'You speak highly of your husband!. How did you come to marry him?'

Abigail smiled, then pulled a face. 'It is a long story, my lord. Believe me, I had no say in the matter'

'I can believe that!'

'But now, since the Lord has kept you, my master, from bloodshed and from avenging yourself on the innocent along with the guilty, may these gifts which your servant has brought to you be given to the men who follow you, and forgive your servant's unwitting offence. The Lord will certainly make for you a lasting dynasty, for you fight the Lord's battles, and let no wrong doing be found in you as long as you live.'

'Amen to that!'

They looked at each other. Then Abigail added softly 'and when the Lord has done every good thing concerning you and has made you leader over Israel, remember your servant.'

She held his gaze a few more moments, then bowed her head.

'I think it unlikely I will ever forget you, or your courage' David said.

The chief steward, who has been watching all this closely nodded, then turned in his saddle and barked orders for the camels to be unloaded.

And so began an impromptu feast out in the desert, at the end of which David's men loaded their horses with more than enough for those waiting for them and started back the way they had come.

The last to part were David and Abigail.

'If you were free, there is so much more I would have to say to you' David told her. And Abigail smiled wistfully.

'But so it must rest between us for the moment' she said. 'You must become King and I must return to a fool!'

David reached out and took her hand for the last time.

'Who knows what the Lord has in store for those who love him?'

He let go, then turned away, mounted his horse and rode away without looking back.

It was dawn when Abigail and the rest returned home and mid-day before Nabal appeared nursing a sore head.

Sore head or not, the chief steward was emboldened to tell him how close they had all come to death the previous night and how it had only been the courage and quick thinking of his mistress which has averted catastrophe.

Nabul's eyes bulged as the details were given and he sunk onto a couch speechless.

And there he lolled for some time until the servant approached again.

He could tell immediately that Nabul had had some kind of fit.

Abigail was summoned and she ordered the servants to carry their master to his bed.

And there he remained unmoving and without speaking again for ten days until finally, when she looked in on him, she saw he was dead.

The news of Nabul's death reached David and he determined to return and ask Abigail to marry him after the prescribed period of mourning.

After David had placed his family under the protection of the King of Moab, they were joined by Zeruiah, the brother of Jesse, David's uncle and his family, having wisely guessed that unable to kill David or punish his immediate family, Saul would seek to revenge himself on anyone connected with him. But Zeruiah's three sons Joab, Abishai and Asahel decided to join David and soon proved themselves outstanding warriors.

Joab, the eldest and strongest was the natural choice for David to send to Abigail when the mourning period was over to enquire on his behalf if a proposal of marriage would be welcome—not that he had many doubts. It was no surprise, then when Joab returned with Abigail's brother who assured David that a great feast would be prepared at the new moon festival and there their father and his entire family would be ready to welcome him.

It was a time of great rejoicing, and for a while David and his men were able to forget that they were fugitives. They would not have felt so much at ease however if anyone had noticed one of Nabul's most favoured servants slip away and ride away to carry the news of David's whereabouts to Saul.

The climax of the feast was the wedding ceremony conducted with great solemnity by Abithar, but once that was over the music and dancing began in earnest and went on long into the night, during which, after a while David and Abigail rode away to an oasis not far away where they could be alone. Only Joab knew where they had gone.

David's wife Michal had been a dutiful wife, but Abigail had no inhibitions and used her body to raise her husband to a level of passion he had never experienced before, and it was dawn before they huddled entwined together under a blanket exhausted but sublimely content.

Two days into the wedding celebrations Saul surrounded the camp with a thousand men.

Despite being heavily outnumbered, Joab and his brothers managed to break out and Joab deliberately led their pursuers in the opposite direction from where he knew David had gone. But as soon as he could, Joab hid in a narrow defile while his brothers continued to lead Saul's men away, and as soon as he was sure they had all gone, he turned back and rode to warn his cousin.

When he realised David had slipped through his fingers yet agaIn, Saul wrecked a terrible revenge on Abigail's family and burned to the ground all the barns and fine buildings Nabul had constructed. Abigail had to be dissuaded from returning 'for surely the King would not harm a mere woman?'

To satisfy her, Joab and David conducted her back under cover of darkness and there she saw the destruction for herself and the bodies, men and women alike whom Saul had put to the sword.

David cursed himself for not having foreseen such a catastrophe. It seemed that anyone he had anything to do with was doomed. But Abigail swore that although she now had nothing but herself to offer him, she would love him to her dying day and asked nothing better than to see him replace the tyrant who had done this.

Chapter eight

Having done what they could to help the few survivors, the three rode to the oasis to meet with Joab's brothers and a few others who had managed to escape. Only two days since it had been a small paradise for two lovers but was now a place of remorse and anger

When David was sure that as many as had escaped had joined them, they set out to ride south, but now it appeared that Saul's eyes were everywhere, having let it be known there would be a rich reward for news of David's whereabouts.

Abigail started to dress like the rest of them, as a group of men with a solitary women was just what Saul would have told his spies to look out for. She also persuaded her new husband to teach her how to handle a sword and under his tuition quickly became good enough to keep the younger cousins on their toes when they practised together—to the amusement of everyone else. But no one could match Joab—not even David.

After many days they reached the great salt lake which was over a thousand feet below the level of the great sea far to the west where there were the Philistine cities of Gaza, Ashdod and Ekron. It was bounded on the western shore by mountains which reared precipitously from the lake side, and these were indented by steep ravines cut into the rock over countless years by streams, some of which still plunged down the mountain sides before reaching the lake. Some of these still contained fish which told of a time long ago when the lake itself was fresh water and they provided drinking water for the few shepherds and their flocks who lived in the many caves, also carved by erosion over the years. It was an ideal place for David and his followers to rest from Saul's pursuit until, hopefully, h e gave up and went home.

But contrary to David's hopes, Saul had no intention of giving up and returning home, a combination of fear and jealousy driving him on.

Accompanied by Abner, the head of his army and three thousand of his most trusted soldiers, he followed information gleaned from various tribesmen—those who would sell their own mothers for a piece of silver. They were a minority, as most loved David and would never have betrayed him, but their information was enough to send Saul in the right direction. And so, one morning, one of the lookouts David had posted at the head of the ravine where they were camped rode down in a hurry to report that he could see large groups of men approaching from both the North and South.

Escape across the lake was impossible owing to its poisonous salinity, but David told the shepherds to tell Saul that was what they had done during the night. And, being unfamiliar with the lake Saul, who met up with Abner leading the other force not far from the entrance to the cave where David and his men had hidden themselves deep in its labyrinthine interior, accepted the story, which was reinforced by discarded clothing and the horses which had been deliberately left for them to find by the lake side.

Exhausted by the pursuit in the extreme heat, Saul decided to make camp and let his men rest. Mules, which carried the provisions, were unloaded on the other side of the ravine from the cave then led forward to drink from the stream in the centre.

Darkness fell and David and Joab crept to the entrance of the cave to assess their chances of escape. But a full moon rose over the mountains behind them and they judged their chances of doing so without disturbing the sleeping camp opposite slim.

They were about to retreat back in the cave when Abishai, Joab's brother, remarked that it was strange Abner seemed to have posted no sentries. And now their eyes were accustomed to the dark, they could see Saul lying beside Abner with all their soldiers lying asleep all round them; evidently, thought to be enough security for the King.

David turned to his companions and said quietly: 'Who will go across to the camp with me?'

'I'll go', said Abishai quickly.

'What for?' Joab said, frowning.

'I don't know. Perhaps I can reason with him'

'Don't be a fool!' Joab growled.

But David was determined. 'You stay here' he said to the rest of them 'If it goes badly you will be able to escape. It's me he wants' Then he turned to Joab:

'I put Abigail under your protection' The big man looked as if to protest again, but finally nodded.

David and Abishai crossed the stream then climbed up to the camp and picked their way quietly past the sleeping soldiers until they were standing directly by Saul and Abner, who had stuck the king's spear into the ground beside where he lay.

Abishai, whispered: 'Today God has given your enemy into your hands. Let me pin him to the ground with his own spear. I won't need to strike him twice.'

He pulled the spear out of the ground but David held up his hand.

'Don't destroy him.' he whispered back. 'Who can lay a hand on the Lord's anointed and be guiltless? As surely as the Lord lives, the Lord himself will strike him. Either his time will come and he will die or he will go into battle and perish. But bring the spear, and get the water jug by his head, then let's go'

When they had crossed the stream again and before they climbed back up to where Joab, Abigail and the others were waiting anxiously, David paused and looked back.

'The Lord forbid that I should lay a hand on the Lord's anointed'

'Then what of these?' Abishai demanded, waiving the spear and jug.

'You will see'

David turned with a half smile as they resumed their climb.

'Get ready to defend yourselves' David said when they were level with the others. Then, taking the spear and jug from Abishai he raised his voice and shouted across the canyon.

'Abner. Abner, Son of Ner. Answer me. I know you can hear me!'

After a few seconds, they heard Abner's voice: 'Who is it who calls me?'.

David shouted: 'Why did you not guard your lord the King? Someone came and could have destroyed him. As surely as the Lord lives you and your men deserve to die because you did not guard your master.'

'What?' Abner growled.

'Look around if you don't believe me. Where are the spear and the water jug that were near the king's head?

They heard Abner curse, but then they heard Saul.

'Is that your voice, David, my son?'

'Yes it is, my lord. And why are you pursuing me? What have I done and what wrong am I guilty of?'

David paused for a moment, then he raised his voice again. 'Listen to me: If the Lord has incited you against me, then maybe he will accept an offering and forgive. But if men have done it, may they be cursed before the Lord for they have driven me from my home and the inheritance which is the right of all our people. My lord, do not let my blood fall to the ground so far from the presence of our God. The king of Israel has come out to look for one blameless—as one hunts a partridge in the mountains!'

There were a few moments silence, and those behind David looked at each other anxiously. Then they heard Saul speak again, but this time quietly, as David had not heard him for many years:

'You are right to rebuke me. I have sinned. Come back to me David my son. Because you have spared my life today. I will not try to harm you again. Surely I have acted like a fool and have erred greatly.'

David nodded and then he said: 'Let one of your young men come over and get the king's spear. The Lord rewards every man for his deeds. He gave you into my hands today but I would not lay a hand on the Lord's anointed. As surely as I valued your life today, so may the Lord value my life and deliver me from my troubles'.

They saw Saul begin to turn away, but then he turned back and raised his hand.

'May you be blessed my son David. You will do great things and surely triumph'

David and the others watched as at dawn Saul and his men struck camp and left. Then there was nothing left of the encounter but some clothing and a few loose horses by the lake side.

Chapter nine

David continued to move around for he said to himself 'One of these days I will be destroyed by Saul who will forget that I spared his life and only remember his jealousy'

After admitting these fears to Abigail, Joab and the others one night as they sat around a fire eating, Joab said: 'The only way we'll get away from Saul for certain is to go and live beyond his kingdom. Then, maybe he'll forget about us'.

David nodded after a few moments. Then he said: 'You're right. But whether he'll forget about us, I'm not so sure!'

Abigail said: 'It will depend on what else he has to think about. But where could we go?'

A discussion followed which ended without an answer to the question. But as David took her into his arms later, she whispered into his ear that she was expecting their first child. And although he was delighted by her news, it made him all the more determined to find a place where they could live in peace for a while.

He lay beside her without sleep long into the night. But a solution presented itself only few weeks later when they learned that the Philistine outpost of Ziklag, a small town on the edge of the desert was being attacked by a substantial force of Arab raiders who sometimes came up from their traditional strongholds in the Negev like a swarm of locusts whenever their own resources were running low and choosing small towns like Ziklag which were poorly defended.

David's relationship with the Philistines was complicated: on the one hand, they knew he was a fugitive from Saul, and therefore seemed to present little threat. Nor were they too concerned whenever he and his followers took refuge on their territory from time to time. But they remembered that he was the one of whom their enemies had sung: 'Saul has slain a thousand Philistines and David ten thousand!'

As long as he stayed away from their cities they left him alone; but kept a watchful eye.

Leaving their families with about a third of their number under the command of Joab's younger brother Asahel to guard the camp, David and Joab rode for the besieged town reaching it just after dark to find the attackers celebrating in their tents having just overcome the town's last resistance.

The inhabitants—men, women and children had been herded into make-shift stockades from which they would be taken in the morning down to the slave markets of Egypt together with all the livestock. The town would then be stripped of anything useful, after which, as was their custom it would be burned to the ground.

David divided their force into two groups and on a given signal attacked the Arab encampment from opposite sides.

Apart from the slaughter inflicted by David and Joab, the Arabs started to fight in the dark amongst themselves. There was little love or trust between the different tribes who had only come together for this raid, and many sprang to the conclusion that members of another group had decided to steal all the loot for themselves.

By dawn, those who had not been killed or wounded had taken to their camels and fled.

David and Joab released the townspeople and helped them back into their homes. The following day, the Philistine Prince Achish, son of Maoch, King of Gath arrived—too late to save the town himself but not to thank David and his men whole heartedly for what they had done. Ziklag was part of Gath and Achish invited them to come to meet his father so that he too could thank them personally.

News of what had happened reached Gath before them and they were greeted by the King with the pomp usually reserved for a visiting prince. But David was aware that despite this, many of those present still looked on him with suspicion.

So when Maoch suggested he brought his followers to live in the city, he politely declined and asked instead if they might live in Ziklag until such time as it was safe for them to return home.

Moach immediately saw the wisdom of this, for living in a border town, David and his men would not only be out of harm's way, but provide a valuable deterrent to any further Arab incursions.

So David returned to Ziklag with his followers and were soon joined by Asahel and the families he had been left to protect. Prince Ashish, who had accompanied David stayed for several days with his attendants, and during this time the two men became firm friends.

Life in the small town returned to normal but the townspeople were delighted when Ashish announced that his father the king had given his permission for David and his followers to stay, and every effort was made to make the newcomers welcome.

Only one person was not completely happy and that was Abigail who, although she was the one to raise the subject that, as was the custom with those who could afford it, her husband was at liberty to take another wife when her pregnancy prevented her fulfilling her duties with the vigour he had come to expect, she had secretly hoped he would dismiss the idea.

The arrival, therefore of Ahinoam, a young woman from Jezreel, caused no little heart ache, which she was at pains to hide, nevertheless. And for her part Ahinoam did everything she could to make Abigail think of her as a younger sister rather than a rival. and became of great comfort to her as the confinement approached.

During this time, David and the others continued to practice with sword, bow and spear knowing that the time would not be long before these skills would be called for again.

To keep their hands in they made periodic raids on the Amalekites to the South and East, thus giving them some of their own medicine and gaining considerable plunder. Much of this David sent back across the border with Saul's kingdom to those sympathetic to him in Hebron, his father's city, and beyond.

They lived like this for a year and four months.

What sparked full scale war again between Saul and the Philistines was never clear to those living in Ziklag, but a messenger arrived from Ascish ordering David to muster his men and join with him against Saul.

This placed them in an agonising dilemma. But fortunately, when King Maoch, heard what his son had done, he called him to the Council Chamber and ordered him to tell David to stay where he was. And although Ascish swore to David's loyalty, the King and his other advisors were adamant not to take the risk that David might take the opportunity of attacking them in the rear during the heat of battle and thus re-establish himself in the eyes of Saul.

Ascish left the meeting in great anger, but had no alternative but to send another message to David telling him to stay where he was.

Within a few days the Philistines had assembled the greatest army seen since the days of Goliath, and this time they were not relying on the intimidation of a champion but a far better armed force who outnumbered Saul's, gathered at Mount Gilboa, by more than two to one.

When Saul saw the gathering Philistine army, he was afraid. He enquired of the Lord, through a priest, but the Lord did not answer him either by dreams or prophesy so he said to his attendants: 'Find me a woman who is a medium so that I may go and enquire of her'.

The servants looked at each other in fear for Saul himself had ordered all the mediums and spiritists banished or put to death. Even to admit to knowing of one was to invite death.

Then one, braver than the rest said: 'I have heard it said there is an old woman in Endor my lord. Whether or not it is true . . . .' his voice trailed away.

Saul said: 'Don't be afraid. Show me where this woman is to be found and you will be richly rewarded'

So, that night, the king disguised himself, and accompanied by only one servant, followed the man to where the old woman lived in a cave.

'Consult a spirit for me', he said offering her a coin,' and bring up for me the one I name'

But the woman said to him: 'Surely you know what Saul has commanded? Why have you set a trap for my life to bring about my death?

Then Saul swore: 'As surely as the Lord lives, you will not be punished for this'

The woman looked at him uncertainly, but the temptation of the money was too great.

'Whom shall I bring up for you?

Saul said: 'Bring me up Samuel'

The woman hesitated, then turned, and closing her eyes began to mutter, until suddenly she cried out at the top of her voice: 'Why have you deceived me. You are Saul!'

But Saul took hold of her arm and said: 'Don't be afraid. What do you see?

The old woman looked at him in terror but he held her firmly.

'Tell me what you see,' he insisted. 'I swear to you, you will come to no harm'

Finally the woman looked past him into the depths of the cave and said fearfully: 'I see a spirit coming up out of the ground!'

Still keeping hold of her, Saul turned to follow her gaze, but saw nothing. and turned back.

'What does he look like?

The woman looked again. Then she said: 'An old man wearing a robe is coming up.'

Then Saul knew it was Samuel and he fell to his knees with his face to the ground.

'Why have you disturbed me by bringing me up?' Saul heard the voice of Samuel, but when he looked up he saw it was the woman who spoke.

Saul bowed his head again and said: 'I am in great distress. The Philistines have come against me with a great army . . . and God has turned away from me. He no longer answers me either by prophets or dreams so I have called on you to tell me what to do.'

He looked up and saw the woman's lips move, but once again, it was the voice of Samuel.

'Why do you consult me now that the Lord has turned away from you and become your enemy? The Lord has done what he predicted through me. He has torn the kingdom out of your hand and given it to another—to David.—because you did not follow his commands and chose your own way. The Lord will hand over both Israel and you to the Philistines and tomorrow you and your sons will be with me.'

On hearing these words Saul fell forwards, full length on the ground filled with terror.

The following day the Philistines surged forward against Saul and the army of Israel. Many died on Mount Gilboa and the invaders pursued those who fled before them. The fighting grew fierce around Saul, Jonathan and his brothers. A few brave men did their best to protect them, but one by one they were overwhelmed.

Finally, Saul was critically wounded by some arrows and he turned to his armour-bearer and said; 'Draw your sword and run me through before they reach us and abuse me'. But the armour bearer was terrified and would not do it. So Saul took his own sword and fell on it.

When the armour bearer saw that the king was dead, he too fell on his sword and died with him. So Saul and his three sons and all those close to them died on the same day.

When the Israelites along the valley and those across the Jordan saw that the Israelite army had fled, and word came that Saul and his sons were dead, they abandoned their towns and fled, so the Philistines came and occupied them.

The following day, when the Philistines were stripping the dead they discovered the bodies of Saul and his three sons. There was great rejoicing in the Philistine camp and messengers were sent back to the cities on coast proclaiming the news.

They cut off Saul's head and fastened his body to the walls of Beth Shan, the nearest Philistine city, but his armour they sent to the temple of the Ashtoreths. They also cut off the heads of Jonathan and his brothers and nailed them to the wall also.

But when the people of Jabesh Gilead, the town Saul had rescued when he first became king, heard what had happened, their foremost warriors travelled through the night and took them down. They took them home where they made a huge funeral pyre and burned them, then they buried their bones under a tamarisk tree after which they mourned for seven days.

David and his men meanwhile had been on another raid into Amalakite territory and knew nothing of this until they returned just as a man arrived from Saul's camp.

His clothes were torn as a sign of mourning, and when he was brought to David he fell at his feet to pay him honour.

'How do you know that Saul and his Son Jonathan are dead?' David demanded.

'I happened to be on Mount Gilboa' the man told him. 'And there was Saul leaning on his spear with the chariots and riders almost upon him. When he saw me he called out to me and I said, 'what can I do?' And he asked me 'who are you?'

'An Amalakite I answered. Then he said 'stand over me and kill me. I am in the throes of death, but I am still alive.' So I stood over him and killed him because I knew that he could not survive'. The man then reached into a sack he had been carrying. 'And I took the crown that was on his head, and the band on his arm'. He held out both to David 'And brought them here to my lord.'

David stared at them for what to those watching seemed a long time, then he turned away, his face contorted with grief.

'Take them from him.' he said to Joab with difficulty.

The man handed them over, clearly taken aback at this turn of events as David turned and walked away.

'But I thought . . .' he stammered

'Go and rest' Joab said gruffly. 'We will call for you later'

He turned and walked after David carrying the crown and band.

He found David in his tent, weeping and soon the whole camp was in mourning—something the Amalakite found mystifying. But he cheered up when later that evening one of David's men came and summoned him.' Surely now he would get the reward he had expected for the story he had concocted when he had found Saul's body before anyone else!'

He found David waiting for him with his men gathered around him.

'You say you are an Amalakite' David said grimly.

'Yes, my lord. I am the son of an alien'

'An enemy!' Joab spat.

The man turned to him fearfully.

David said, 'The Amalakites have been enemies of Israel since we came up out of Egypt and they attacked us rather than let us go on our way peacefully.'

'And never ceased to fight against us whenever they thought they had a chance of plunder' Joab added. 'How do we know you are not lying now? How do we know you didn't just happen to find the King and made the whole thing up, hoping for a reward?

'The Amalakte began to look terrified.

'Oh no my lord, he stammered. 'I killed him, I swear'.

David said: 'If you speak the truth, why were you not afraid to lift your hand to destroy the Lord's anointed. Something I myself dared not do?'

'But . . .'

David glanced at one of those standing close by.

'Strike him down,

'No!' the Amalakite shrieked, falling to his knees. 'Mercy'

David's man thrust his sword into the man's body and he fell forward.

David looked down at him.

'Your blood be on your own head when you said 'I killed the Lord's anointed.'

Some young men came forward and took the body of the Amalakite to be buried.

Then David turned to look at those around him and said: 'Saul and Jonathan are dead. It's time for us to go home'.

Chapter ten

David and his wives, Abigail and Ahinoam, together with Joab and his brothers, and all those who had been with him at Ziklag with their families set out for their home town of Hebron. Some, without family responsibilities rode ahead so that as the main body approached the town, David's parents and brothers, who had returned from Moab when they heard of Saul's death, rode out to meet him with many of the Town's elders and conducted him the remaining miles until they were met by all the people of the town amidst great rejoicing.

That very day he was anointed King of Judah.

When David heard that it had been the people of Jabesh Gilead who had buried Saul and his sons he sent a message to them saying: 'The Lord bless you for showing this kindness to Saul your master. May the Lord show you too his kindness, and I will also show you the same because you did this. Now do not lose heart because Saul is dead, because the house of Judah has anointed me King over them'.

In the meantime, Abner, Commander of Saul's army, who had managed to fight his way through the encircling Philistines with some of his personal guard and so escaped the slaughter on Mount Gilboa, gathered whatever survivors were left who could still ride a horse or mule, and taking Ish Bosheth, the remaining Son of Saul who was lame with him, travelled to the North beyond the reach of the Philistines, and there at Mahanaim made him King over the Northern Tribes, including Gilead on the other side of the Jordan. Ish Bosheth was forty years old when he became King over Israel and he reigned for two years

In time, when Abner had rebuilt the army of Israel, he felt strong enough to challenge David for the Kingdom of Judah and set out to march South. Word of this reached Hebron and David gathered the army of Judah and marched out to meet him.

The two armies camped opposite each other at Gibeon and David sent Joab forward with an escort under a flag of truce to meet Abner and see if there was not some way of avoiding further bloodshed.

Abner also came forward with some of his men and they met at the pool of Gibeon where they sat down on either side of the pool opposite each other.

Then Abner said,' why should we engage the armies in battle? Let twelve of your young men fight twelve of ours hand to hand, and let the King to whom the defeated belong acknowledge the other as King over all of us.'

Joab agreed to this, and each side counted off twelve champions who then drew their daggers and fought their opposite number. But in a short space of time all taking part were badly wounded and fell to the ground.

When David saw what had happened, he ordered the trumpets to sound for battle and the main armies closed on each other.

The fighting was fierce, but as the day drew to a close David and his warriors pushed the opposing army back until suddenly it collapsed and Abner's men turned tail and ran for their lives.

Asahel, youngest brother of Joab was there. He could out run anyone and set off after Abner turning neither to left or right. Abner eventually paused for breath and looking back saw the young man coming up behind him, and as he got closer Abner could see who it was and shouted: 'Is that you Asahel?'

'It is' The other stopped some fifty yards away.

Abner said: 'Don't follow me. Choose someone else and strip him of his weapons.' But Asahel drew his short sword and started walking towards him.

'Don't be a fool!' Abner growled. 'Why should I strike you down? How could I look your brother Joab in the face?'

But Asahel drew ever closer

Abner turned as if to run away, but at the last moment, when Asahel was almost upon him, and without turning, Abner thrust his spear backwards into the young man's stomach with such force it came out of his back, and he fell to the ground.

Joab and Abishai pursued Abner, and as the sun was setting they came to a hill where the survivors of the tribe of Benjamin—Saul's people—rallied behind Abner and formed themselves into a group on the crest.

Joab waited for more of his own men to join him, but before he gave the order to attack Abner shouted: 'Must we fight each other forever? Don't you realise this will end in lasting bitterness? How long before you order your men to stop pursuing their brothers?'

Joab looked at Abishai who said: 'What he says is true. More bloodshed can only delay the day when all Israel accepts David'.

After a second, Joab nodded, then he turned and shouted back up the hill: 'As surely as God lives, if you had not spoken, we would have continued our pursuit. Very well then. Go in peace . . . . for now,' he added softly, looking at Abishai.

Then he turned to those behind him and waved them back. Some were disappointed, but all turned obediently and began the journey back to re-join the others

When he was sure it was not a trick, Abner gave a signal and he and those with him went down the hill on the opposite side and continued on their way.

All that night, Abner and his men marched north until they reached Mahanaim where Ish Bosheth was waiting anxiously.

When Joab and the others arrived, David ordered a count to be made of those killed and wounded. Besides Asahel, nineteen of their own were found dead and three hundred and sixty who were with Abner.

David ordered that all should be buried with full honour, but Asahel they took and buried in his father's tomb in Bethlehem. Then they marched all night joining the others at Hebron at day break.

The war between the house of Saul and the House of David lasted a long time, but gradually David became stronger and Ish Bosheth weaker. Despite this, Abner strengthened his own position so that increasingly people looked to him rather than the King.

Things came to a head when Rizpah, who had been a concubine of Saul and was still a beautiful woman, came to Abner one night and declared her love for him. She stayed with him that night and from then on became his constant companion News of this soon reached the King's ears and it was pointed out to him by one of his advisors that for Abner to take his father's concubine was to declare himself on a level with the King himself.

Ish Bosheth was a weak man, but like many such, impulsive and liable to speak without thinking of the consequences.

Surrounding himself with councillors, he summoned Abner and demanded that he gave up Rizpah and swore never to have anything more to do with her again.

He did not get to deliver the judgement he next planned for Rizpah herself, as Abner immediately flew into a rage and demanded to know if the King thought he was a dog to be spoken to like that. It was he who had put Ish Bosheth on the throne and now he would see how long his rule would last when he took away his support; he and all his pet cronies who had no more strength between them to lift a blade of grass, never mind a sword!

All eyes followed him fearfully as he stormed out of the meeting and rode away.

Shortly afterwards, Abner sent a messenger to David: 'Whose land is it?' the scroll conveyed to David said. 'Make an agreement with me and I will help bring all Israel over to you'.

David was so delighted he did not wait to consult Joab, who was away with his brother Abishai driving back a Philistine raiding party, and sent the messenger back with an immediate reply:

'Tell your master I will make an agreement, but I demand one thing of him: not to come into my presence unless he brings Michal daughter of Saul when he comes to see me; she who was my wife before her father took her away and gave her to Paltiel son of Laish'

Abner nodded contentedly when he heard David's reply and immediately sent men to bring Michal to him. Her husband followed her down the road weeping, until told to go home if he valued his life.

Before going to see David, Abner conferred with the elders of Israel, including leaders from Saul's own tribe, the Benjaminites.

When they had all gathered, Abner stood up and spoke to them:

'For some time you have wanted to make David your King. Now do it! For the Lord promised through the prophet: 'By my servant David I will rescue my people Israel from the hand of the Philistines and from the hand of all their enemies'.

Then, with all in agreement, Abner with twenty supporters travelled to Hebron taking Michal with them to tell David everything the northern tribes, including the house of Benjamin, were willing to do.

David prepared a feast, at the end of which, Abler rose and proposed a toast to 'the future king of all Israel!'.

'Let us go at once to call a great assembly for you my Lord that they may make a compact with you and that you may rule over all that your heart desires'

So David sent them on their way in peace to await the promised summons.

That night, not long after this, Joab and Abishai returned with all the soldiers who had been with them and a great deal of plunder recovered from the Philistines. They were told that Abner had come to the king and that David had received him with honour and sent him on his way in peace.

Seething with anger, Joab went at once to the king.

'Why have you done this?' he demanded. 'Why did you let him go? You know Abner, son of Ner. He came to deceive you; to observe your movements and find out everything you are doing Have you forgotten that he murdered your cousin, my brother?!'

It had been a long time since anyone had dared to speak to David like that and others present looked on aghast. But as David rose to his feet to confront Joab, the other turned on his heel and strode from the room.

Joab set out at once after Abner with some of his best warriors. He also sent a messenger ahead on a swift horse, asking Abner to wait as the king had a further message.

The messenger caught up with Abner and his companions who promptly dismounted when they received the message to wait. And when Joab and the others arrived Abner walked to greet them smiling

Joab also dismounted then drew Abner into the cover of some trees as if to impart a private word from David. And there, Joab stabbed him in the stomach so he fell to the ground. Then he and his men struck down the rest and threw their bodies with Abner into a deep well nearby where those not already dead perished instantly.

When David heard of this he was appalled; not only because of the brutality of the act itself but the fatal damage it might do to their hope of reconciliation with the rest of Israel, and he hastened to make a pronouncement:

'I and my kingdom are forever innocent before the Lord concerning the blood of Abner and his men. May his blood fall upon the head of Joab and his father's house'

Then he ordered Joab and all the people with him to put on sack cloth and walk in mourning behind Abner's coffin. David himself put on sack cloth and walked with them.

They buried Abner in Hebron. Then the king and all the people mourned for thirty days.

The Northern tribes, including the tribe of Benjamin, took note of this and were satisfied. Indeed, everything the King did pleased them and they accepted that David had no part in the murder. But David confided to his wives that although he was king he dared not move Joab from his command of the army. 'But may the Lord repay him for his evil deeds'

Then Abigail, who was the wisest said: 'You are right, my Lord. My people have a saying 'keep your friends close . . . . and your enemies closer!'

When Ish-Bosheth, son of Saul heard that Abner was dead, he lost courage. All his supporters were alarmed and many deserted him.

Two of these were violent men—leaders of raiding bands— Baanah and his brother Recab. They agreed between them that their master's cause was lost and if they were not to end on the losing side they had better do something to ingratiate themselves with David. So they set out for the house of Ish-Bosheth without telling anyone. They arrived in the heat of the day when the king was taking his afternoon rest.

Telling the servants they had an urgent message for the king, they went into the inner part of the house; quietly entered the bed chamber, then plunged their daggers into the sleeping man's stomach as he was lying on the bed, killing him instantly and without a sound. They cut off his head, and taking it with them, strode out of the house and made their escape.

They travelled all night and eventfully reached Hebron where they brought the king's head to David and laid it in front of him as he sat surrounded by his councillors and bodyguard.

'Here is the head of the son of Saul, your enemy who tried to take your life' the elder one boasted. 'This day the Lord has avenged David against Saul and his offspring'

David rose to his feet, and the brothers looked at him expectantly. But David said:

'As surely as the Lord lives who has delivered me out of all trouble, when a man told me, 'Saul is dead,' and thought he was bringing me good news, I seized him and put him to death.' The two brothers glanced at each other anxiously as David went on:

'That was the reward I gave him for his news! How much more, when two wicked men come and tell me they have killed an innocent man in his own house and on his own bed, should I not now demand his blood at their hands and rid the earth of them?'

David glanced at those beside him and nodded, and without another word they dragged the two brothers outside who were now screaming for mercy.

Abishai glanced down at the head of Ish-Bosheth and said: 'What of this, my Lord?'

David thought for a moment, then he sighed and said quietly: 'Let it be buried with honour in the tomb of Abner.'

After this, all the Tribes of Israel came to David at Hebron and said: 'We are your own flesh and blood. In the past, while Saul was king, you were the one who led Israel on their military campaigns. And the Lord said to you, 'you shall shepherd my people Israel and you shall become their ruler.'

So David made a compact with them at Hebron, and he became king over all Israel.

He was thirty years old when he became king and he reigned for forty years.

Chapter eleven

After seven years had passed, David became aware that although the other tribes of Israel were loyal to him, they were increasingly unhappy that he stayed in Hebron, the city of Judah

He called a meeting of his advisors, and it was agreed that he should establish his capital in a neutral city. And after further discussion, David chose Jerusalem, a substantial and well fortified city occupied by the Jebusites who, although surrounded by land belonging to the twelve tribes, had resisted all attempts to eject them. The city was virtually impregnable by reason of its position on a hill top, and walls which had been built up over the years to the most formidable then known.

Even so, it was ideal, if only it could be taken; so preparations began.

A few weeks later, David arrived with his army at the foot of the hill on which Jerusalem stood. With Joab and a small detachment, he climbed to just beneath the walls and shouted to those on top who had watched his approach to fetch the rulers of the city as he would like to offer a truce.

When the rulers duly appeared, David offered to let them remain in the city unharmed as long as they opened the gates to him. But this drew jeers and ribald laughter.

'You won't get in here' they shouted back. 'Even the blind and lame could ward you off!'

A few threw rocks which only just missed them, and this was followed by even more laughter and jeers as those on the walls watched David and his party retreat down the hill.

Joab was fuming with anger and swore what he would do to their tormentors when he got hold of them. But David warned him to calm down. What was needed was a strategy not loss of temper.

For the rest of the day, they rode slowly right around the city—which was indeed formidable. A long siege seemed inevitable, but that would be costly, both in lives and material. But in the late afternoon, they noticed a stream gushing from a place not far from the walls on the north side. Closer inspection revealed the water to be emerging from a small cave the entrance of which was hidden by some bushes and which seemed to have been carved by human hands—possibly as an outflow to a source within the city.

As soon as he realised this, David led those with him on, stopping at other places so that those watching from the walls would not think they had noticed anything significant. But after dark, they returned and discovered the water outlet was big enough for a man to wriggle through if he did not mind getting wet and that it ended after a hundred yards at the foot of a shaft which undoubtedly led up into the city.

The following day, out of sight of the city walls, David and his men prepared to scale the water shaft. When it grew dark again, smaller men who were good climbers were chosen to lead the way with ropes to assist those who came on behind—a select group led by Joab's brother Abishai. Only ten men were thought to be needed as all they had to do was break out of the top of the shaft and run to the main gate to open it for the rest of the army who would be waiting out of sight.

The plan went well to start with, but climbing with only the aid of flares at the foot of the shaft, the leader lost his grip and fell to the bottom dislodging three who were on their way up behind him.

Their place was taken by Abishai himself and two others and these managed to reach the top without further incident.

The shaft was covered by a grill. They started to lift this out of the way and help the rest to follow, but they were seen by one of the guards on the wall behind them, who gave the alarm. But before reinforcements arrived, the intruders ran to the gate, and after a short skirmish, over powered the gate keepers and unbarred and swung open the gates.

They were about to be overwhelmed by a force of defenders who ran towards them, but just before they arrived, David and Joab burst through and the fight spread out across the now terror struck city.

By morning, everything was quiet. David had those leaders who had spurned his offer and who still survived to be executed and the other survivors were given two days to gather their belongings and leave—except for the young unmarried women who were given as wives to any of his soldiers who wanted them.

When the Philistines heard that David had been anointed King over all Israel and was in Jerusalem they came up in full force to search for him. But a messenger from an outpost on the border which Joab had established, fully expecting such a development, reached the King a full day's march in front of the invading army.

David left sufficient men under the command of Abishai to defend the city if the invading army broke through, while he and Joab led the rest to meet them.

It was almost dark by the time they reached the end of a gorge which opened out onto the plain of Rephaima, a place from which they could see, without being seen, the enemy army who were spread out over the whole valley in front of them.

The Philistines had evidently camped for the night with a view to attacking Jerusalem the following day when they were fully rested and ready for battle.

It was an awesome sight. David and his men were clearly outnumbered several times over, and they knew the enemy to be savage and skilled warriors, heavily armed with bronze shields and iron weapons of all kinds, more advanced than anything they possessed themselves.

Joab advised David against a night attack as their own men were tired and the enemy so spread out they would risk getting separated from each other in the dark. David agreed, and that night they camped without lighting any fires that would have given away their presence.

Early the following morning, and while it was still dark he went to Nathan the prophet who had travelled with them and asked him to enquire of the Lord.

'Shall I attack the Philistines or should we return and help to defend the City? Will you hand them over to me?'

Nathan closed his eyes while David waited for what seemed an eternity.

Then without opening them Nathan said: 'Go, for I will surely hand them over to you. But do not meet them face to face. Circle around them while it is still dark and attack them from a direction they are not expecting. Wait by the balsam trees you will find there until you hear the sound of marching feet in the tops of the trees, then move quickly because that will mean the Lord has gone out in front of you to strike down the Philistine army'.

David did as commanded. When he heard the marching of feet, he rose with Joab and all his men and fell upon the enemy defeating them with a great slaughter and pursuing the survivors back into their cities on the coast

News of this great victory preceded them so that when they returned to Jerusalem, everyone came out to meet them, and that night there was a great celebration.

Chapter twelve

After the rout of the Philistines, David received messengers from Hiram king of Tyre, whose people were renowned for their skill as builders and had access to the forests of Lebanon which were rich in precious woods of all kinds. Hiram had established friendly relations with David soon after he became king of Judah and the messengers brought a letter from him congratulating him on his victory, for the Philistines were also bitter enemies of Tyre, and offering not only to send him skilled carpenters and stone masons to build him a suitable palace, but to supply all the cedar logs that would be required.

It was an exciting time for all the inhabitants of Jerusalem not least David's wives who were given charge of the design of the quarters intended for them.

David reigned over all Israel doing what was right and just and he was loved and trusted by all the the people. To help him in the heavy responsibilities that fell on his shoulders, in addition to his cousin Joab, whom he confirmed as commander of his army, he made Jehosaphat, a wise and honest man of the tribe of Benjamen who had served Saul, his chief minister. He was getting on in years, but David valued his experience and knew he could trust him implicitly. He also appointed Seraiah, a younger man from his own tribe as his private Secretary and finally Ahimelech, who had been with him in his wanderings from the beginning, and Zadok, a Levite from the priestly line of Aaron, the brother of Moses, chief priests.

In addition to these, other trustworthy men were appointed to David's court who had rallied to his cause long before it had been safe to do so.

As was the custom, David took more wives and concubines, and sons and daughters were born to him. But it was to Abigail he never failed to turn whenever he needed rest from the duties of kingship, or wise council besides that offered by his officials who, apart from Joab and those others who had been with him from the beginning, he suspected sometimes of yielding too easily when they thought they had his mind on some matter.

Shortly after the Royal Palace was completed, David called a meeting of all his officials and announced that the Ark of the Covenant, the most holy of all objects which the Israelites had carried through the desert from Mount Sinai and in which Moses had placed the tablets on which God himself had written the Ten Commandments, was to be brought up from the house of Abinadab on a hill where it had rested since it was recovered from the Philistines during the time of the Samuel.

A Tent of Meeting, a copy of the one the Israelites had also carried through the desert and which would house the Ark was made and erected not far from the new Palace.

David, with thirty thousand chosen men accompanied the priests and Levites; the only ones permitted to carry the Ark, as it was brought up into the city which was packed with every man, woman and child who were able to make the journey to Jerusalem.

Hundreds of musicians played and countless choristers made a great shout as the Levites with their precious burden arrived at the entrance of the Tent where the King himself and his family danced in celebration.

The Ark was placed by the priests on a stand prepared to receive it in an inner part of the great canopy out of sight of all but they themselves, but the celebrations went on for many hours until David blessed the people and sent them home with a loaf of bread for every family as well as a cake of dates and a cake of raisons.

Only one person did not celebrate: Michal, Saul's daughter and David's first wife who had looked down on her husband from a window in the Palace dancing in celebration and despised him in her heart.

She went out to meet him as he returned.

'How the king of Israel has distinguished himself today, disrobing and dancing in the sight of the slave girls of his servants like any common person!' she scolded.

David answered quietly: 'It was before the Lord I chose to dance—he who chose me rather than your father or any in his family when he appointed me ruler over his people. So I will celebrate before him. I will become even more undignified. I might even be humiliated in my own eyes . . . . but by those slave girls you so despise, I will be held in honour'

So saying he turned on his heel and walked past her without a backward glance.

They never spoke again.

After the King was settled in his Palace, the Lord gave him rest from all his enemies.

One day, he sent for Nathan the Prophet and said: 'Here am I living in a palace of cedar while the Ark of God remains in a tent!

'Nathan smiled. Then he said: 'Whatever you have in mind, go ahead, for the Lord is with you.

But when the King rose early the following morning, he found Nathan already waiting for him and asked what could have so disturbed his rest.

Nathan said: 'Last night the Lord spoke to me. He said 'Go tell my servant David, are you the one to build a house for me to dwell in? I have not dwelt in a house from the day I brought the Israelites up out of Egypt to this day. Wherever I moved with them, did I ever say to any of their rulers whom I commanded to shepherd my people, 'why have you not built me a house of cedar?' So tell my servant David, I took you from the pasture and from following your father's flock to be a ruler over my people. I have been with you where-ever you have gone and I have cut down all your enemies before you. Now I will make your name great, like the greatest men of the earth, and I will provide a place for my people Israel so they can have a home of their own and no longer be disturbed. I will also give you rest from all your enemies. I myself will establish a house for you and when your days are over and you rest with your fathers, I will raise up a son to succeed you, and I will establish his Kingdom. He is the one who will build a house for me and I will establish the throne of his kingdom for ever. I will be his father, and he will be my son. My love will never be taken away from him.'

Nathan paused, then he said: 'This is what the Lord told me to tell you.'

Then he turned on his heel and left.

David watched him go. Then, taking no one with him, he walked to the entrance of the Tent of Meeting.

The three priests on duty prostrated themselves when they recognised him but after a brief word he walked past them and through to the inner part of tent where the Ark was resting. The three glanced at each other anxiously. It was not permitted for anyone other than the chief priest to enter the sanctum, but none had the courage to challenge him. He was the King after all.

David closed the flap separating the sanctum from the rest of the tent then he fell on his knees before the Ark and began to pray aloud with outstretched hands so that although the priests could not see him, they heard him clearly.

'How great you are O Sovereign Lord 'David prayed.' There is no one like you and no God but you. You have revealed this to your servant, saying 'I will build a house for you'. So your servant has found courage to offer you this prayer. Now be pleased to bless the house of your servant that it may continue forever in your sight, for you O Lord have spoken and with your blessing, the house of David will be blessed forever.'

Then David prostrated himself before the Ark and remained for a long time while the priests stood with heads bowed at the entrance. Others arrived to worship but were kept back as long as the King remained, so word quickly spread that the King was worshipping before the Lord. This pleased the people and they gathered at the Tent of Meeting to greet the King with shouts of approval when he finally emerged.

It was not known at the time, not even by David himself, but this moment was the closest David was ever to feel to the one who had brought him thus far, and It was not long before he was put to the test.

Chapter thirteen

In the Spring, when the weather generally favoured military campaigns, David sent Joab out with his commanders and the whole army to subdue the Ammonites who had again started sending raiding parties across the border. But he did not go with them having several matters of administration that required his close attention.

One late afternoon, he got up from the couch where he had been taking a rest during the heat of the day and started to stroll around the roof of the palace enjoying the view of the City in the cool of the day and listening to the sounds of the street traders coming from below as they set out their stalls for the evening trade. Merchants came from a considerable distance to Jerusalem these days as the city had enjoyed a period of peace under David's protection longer than any could remember and the people had grown prosperous.

David smiled as he looked down. Trade was preferable to war and he knew his officials would make sure the proper tax was collected from those enjoying the opportunities offered to make a good profit.

He eventfully reached the side facing a quieter district, and there on the roof of a house close by, he saw a woman bathing attended by a young girl The woman was very beautiful, and after a moment's hesitation David called a servant and sent him to find out about her.

The man returned and reported that her name was Bathsheba, the daughter of Eliam a minor official and wife to Uriah, a Hittite Officer who was away with Joab at the war. later, Bathsheba was attending to some household records seated under a small tree in the centre of a courtyard at the back of the house when her servant came out to tell her that a royal official accompanied by two soldiers was at the front door and wished to speak with her.

Bathsheba stood up in alarm. It could only mean they brought news of her husband.

She waited trembling while the girl went to fetch the men to whom she bowed low when they appeared. Then, unable to contain herself blurted out: 'Uriah. You have brought news of my husband. Is he dead?'

It seemed she was about to faint, and the official reached forward quickly and took her hand

'Please, my lady, it is nothing like that. There is no need to be alarmed' He helped her to stand up, and now, facing her, saw how beautiful she was; could not be more than twenty years old, and Uriah twice that age; indeed, a lucky man!

'Your husband is well' he told her, 'and highly thought of by my Lord, Joab'.

Bathsheba looked at him puzzled. 'Then why have you come?' she asked.

The official took a breath, then he said. 'My Lord the King has heard of your beauty, and bids me to invite you to the palace this very night so that he might satisfy himself that the reports are true.'

Bathsheba hesitated, then she said: 'The King wants to see me?'

The official nodded.

Bathsheba glanced at her maid, who looked back at her giving a slight shrug.

Bathsheba made up her mind.

'Tell the King I will be honoured to attend with my servant. But first I must prepare myself.'

'I understand' the official nodded.

'Tell him. I will come in two hours time'.

'I am instructed to escort you immediately.'

But Bathsheba looked at him levelly.

'He will understand. If it is my appearance he wishes to judge, he must give me the opportunity to make the best of myself.'

She held the official's gaze for a few moments, then the man gave a bow.

'I will tell the King. If he still wants to see you, I will call again in two hours time'

So saying, he turned on his heel, and followed by the soldiers, swept out while the two women bowed low in obeisance.

When they had gone, both women straightened up, and the maid giggled.

'Do you really intend to go?

Bathsheba nodded. 'You don't insult the King.' She paused, then smiled. 'But he must not think I am some trollop he can pick up as he pleases, even if he is the King!'

The girl giggled again. 'And if he likes you?' she said archly.

'Do you mean, if he wants to take me to his bed?'

'Yes'.

Bathsheba paused, then smiled again.

'Did you not see him dance before the Ark of the Lord?'

'Of course'

'And did you not think him handsome?'

'He is very handsome, my lady. Any woman would enjoy being joined to one such as he.'

'They say there are many women in the palace besides his three wives.'

'So I have heard.'

Bathsheba looked defiant.

'If he wants me, he must love me.'

The maid hesitated, then she said: 'And what of my Master?'

Bathsheba paused for quite a long time, then she said quietly. 'We shall see.'

David was not pleased with the message his official brought back. He was not used to being kept waiting by a mere woman. But he was even more intrigued to see her at close quarters. And when she finally appeared, dressed in her finest robe and with her long dark hair skilfully arranged to best advantage, his irritation fled.

He entertained her with wine and choice foods. Then he dismissed all the attendants apart from some musicians who played softly in the courtyard below.

When they had gone and they were alone together Bathsheba stood up and slipping her robe from her shoulders stood before him naked.

'Is this what you want, your majesty?

David took her in his arms.

'Yes', he said wonderingly. 'But I did not expect to receive it so quickly. Bathsheba laughed softly.

'I did not feel it polite to keep the King waiting twice in one day!'

They made love until daybreak the following day, her body meeting his with equal passion and presenting herself to him with seemingly unending invention until they fell asleep exhausted but still entwined.

Never had the King felt so enthralled, and he sent her home with costly gifts. But a few weeks later, she sent him a message, telling him that she was pregnant.

David immediately sent word to Joab asking that he send Uriah the Hittite with a report of the fighting, and when Uriah arrived he was shown into the presence of the King who asked him how Joab was, how the soldiers were and how the war was going.

Uriah gave him his report and told the King that they were now besieging Rabbah, the Ammonite Capital and the last Ammonite City to resist capture.

David listened attentitively, then he rose, and congratulating Uriah on the clarity of his report told him to go down to his house, where his wife was undoubtedly eagerly waiting for him, and enjoy himself; and he sent a gift of wine after him.

But Uriah did not go to his house but slept instead at the entrance to the palace with his master's servants.

When David was told this, he sent for Uriah and asked him why he had not gone home.

Uriah answered: 'The Ark is staying in a tent and my master Joab and all my lord's men are camped in open fields. How could I go to my house to eat and drink and lie with my wife?. As surely as you live, my lord, I could not do such a thing'

Then David said to him,' very well. Stay here one more day and tomorrow I will send you back'

So Uriah remained in Jerusalem that day and the next. At David's invitation, he ate and drank with him and David made him drunk. But in the evening Uriah went out to sleep on his mat among the servants and still did not go home.

Then, driven by exasperation and fear, David did something he was to regret for the rest of his life, but for the moment his mind was filled with thoughts of Bathsheba and the need to protect her from the stoning that would be her certain fate if her husband returned to find his wife had betrayed him. He wrote a sealed letter to Joab and sent it with Uriah. In it he wrote: 'Put Uriah in the front line where the fighting is fiercest. Then withdraw from him so that he will be struck down and die'.

So while Joab had the city under siege, he put Uriah at a place where he knew the strongest defenders were, and when the men of the city came out and fought against Joab, some of the men in David's army fell, and Uriah died among them.

Joab sent a full account of the battle to David and he instructed the messenger: 'When you have finished giving your account, the King's anger may flare up and he may ask you 'why did you get so close to the city? Didn't you realise they would shoot arrows from the wall? If he asks you this, then say to him, 'Also, your servant Uriah the Hittite is dead'.

So the messenger set out, and when he arrived he told David everything Joab had instructed him to say, including that Uriah the Hittite was dead.

If he had been an observant man, he might have thought to himself that the king seemed to take the news of Uriah's death remarkably well.

David then sent a message back to Joab saying: 'Don't let this upset you. The sword devours one as well as another. Press the attack against the city and destroy it.' The king paused for a moment, before adding: 'Yes, say that to Joab to encourage him'.

When Uriah's wife heard that her husband was dead, she mourned for him.

But after the time of mourning was over, David had her brought to the palace and she became his wife and bore him a son.

But the thing that David had done had not gone unseen.

Nathan appeared at the palace shortly after Bathsheba's son was born. Thinking the Prophet had called to congratulate him, the King put aside the documents presented to him by his Secretary and ordered that he be admitted without delay.

'What can I do for you my old friend' he said affably when Nathan entered and offered him a chair by his own. But Nathan continued to stand.

'I have something to tell you' he said without returning the king's smile. David frowned momentarily, but gestured with his hand for him to continue.

'There were two men in a certain town,' Nathan began, 'one rich, the other poor. The rich man had large numbers of sheep and cattle, but the poor man had nothing except one little ewe lamb that he had bought. He raised it and it grew up with him and his children. It shared his food, drank from his cup, and even slept in his arms. It was like a daughter to him.'

David frowned again, but nodded, and Nathan continued: 'Now a traveller came to the rich man, but the rich man refrained from taking one of his own sheep or cattle to prepare a meal for his visitor. Instead, he took the ewe lamb that belonged to the poor man and prepared it for his guest.'

David started to his feet in anger. 'As surely as the Lord lives, the man who did this deserves to die! He must pay four times over for doing such a thing and had no pity'

Nathan looked at him, then he said: 'You are that man. And this is what the Lord, the God of Israel says: 'I anointed you King over Israel, and I delivered you from the hand of Saul. I gave your master's house to you and your master's wives into your arms. I gave you the Houses of Israel and Judah. And if all this had been too little, I would have given you more. Why did you despise the Lord by doing what is evil in his eyes? You struck down Uriah the Hittite as surely as if by your own sword and took his wife to be your own. Now, therefore, the sword shall never depart from your house because you despised me and took that which was not yours. Out of your own household I am going to bring calamity upon you. Before your very eyes I will take your wives from you and give them to one who is close to you, and he will lie with them in broad daylight. You did it in secret, but I will do this before all Israel.'

After a moment, David fell on his knees before Nathan with his head hung in shame.

'I have indeed sinned against the Lord and deserve to die. Let him take my life.'

'You are not going to die' Nathan answered more gently. 'But because by doing this you have encouraged the enemies of the Lord to show contempt for his word, the son born to you will die.'

As soon as he had gone, David hurried to Bathsheba's quarters to see his son and was relieved to see him in perfect health. Despite this, he slept fitfully that night and early the following morning prostrated himself in the Tent of Meeting asking the Lord to take his life instead of that of the child. But the boy fell ill and several nights later, a wail of such despair echoed through the palace that none failed to hear, or recognise a mother crying aloud for her child

David ran to his wife's room and found her kneeling by the boy's cot, surrounded by her attendants.

One glance was enough to tell him the child was dead.

David did what he could to comfort Bathsheba, and in due course she became pregnant again.

Meanwhile, Joab was still fighting against the Ammonite city of Rabbah. In time he captured the royal citadel, after which he sent an urgent message to David saying: 'I have taken the city's water supply. Now muster the rest of the troops and besiege the city and capture it, otherwise I shall take the city and it will be named after me.'

So David mustered the entire army and attacked, and captured it.

Joab took the crown from the head of their King which was made of gold and encrusted with precious stones and placed it on David's head.

The survivors of the defenders were rounded up and consigned to labour with axes and iron picks or brick making. But the Ammonite King and his family were put to death.

The army stripped the town of all it contained and returned to Jerusalem with a great deal of plunder.

David himself had even more to celebrate: Abigail met him and told him that Bathsheba had given birth to a son in his absence and was waiting eagerly in her chambers to present the child to him. David turned and hurried away watched by a smiling Abigail.

'Nathan is there too', she called after him.'

David stopped abruptly and swung back to face her.

'It's all right' she assured him. 'Go'.

David continued on his way, and despite her assurance entered the room anxiously.

Nathan smiled and Bathsheba bowed low before leading him to a small crib and drew back a light cover to reveal his new son to him. Then she picked him up and placed him in David's arms.

Nathan came up beside them 'He is a beautiful child' he murmured, and because the Lord loves him is destined for greatness., David looked back at his wife fondly.

'Do you have name for him?'

Bathsheba nodded. 'If my lord permits, I would like to call him Solomon'

David nodded. 'Solomon is a good name'

Nathan said, 'He shall be Solomon, but he shall also be known as Jedidiah—which means 'loved by the Lord'.

David lifted the little boy high above his head laughing.

'Two important names, for such a small person!'

The others joined in his laughter

Chapter fourteen

Years passed. David continued to rule Israel wisely and with compassion. He was loved by the people and the Lord continued to give him rest from his enemies.

He took more wives and concubines and had sons and daughters of whom he was justly proud, and in time his elder sons became close advisors. If he remembered the prophesy of Nathan he put it to one side and most of the time gave it little thought. But in time Amnon, his eldest son, fell in love with Tamar, the daughter of David's wife Maacah and the sister of his second son, Absolom. Tamar was very beautiful. But, being his half sister, and sister of Absalom, who surpassed him both in appearance and ability—probably their father's favourite among the elder brothers, Amnon could not see how he could ever possess her, and in time, this made him ill.

But he had a friend at court; Jonadab, son of Shimeah, David's brother. Jonadab was a very shrewd man, and he eventually challenged Amnon.

'Why do you the king's son look so haggard morning after morning?'

Amnon pulled a face. Then he shook his head and said: 'It is Tamar, my brother's sister. I long to possess her. To run my fingers through her hair and cover her naked body with kisses, but I know such a thing is impossible. So I am dying of longing. Without her, my life is not worth living!'

'Is that all?' Jonadab said smiling. 'Then listen to me, and I will tell you how you may gain your heart's desire'.

Ammon looked at his friend eagerly as he continued. 'Go to bed and pretend to be ill.'

'I won't have to pretend!'

'All the better. Your father will hear of it and is bound to be concerned for you. So, when he comes to see you and asks if there is anything you need, say to him, 'I would like my sister Tamar to come and give me something to eat. The two friends looked at each other, then both laughed.

'And when she is sent, you will know what to do!'

So Amnon did as his friend suggested, and sure enough the king soon hurried to go and see him.

'I would like my sister Tamar to prepare some food in my sight so I can watch her and then eat it from her hand.' Amnon said weakly

The king might normally have wondered at this request, but such was his concern, all else was forgotten.

'Perhaps she could make some special bread in my sight?' Amnon went on.

David put his hand on his son's forehead and nodded.

'It shall be as you ask'.

'Thank you father'

David nodded again. Then he left the room without looking back. Had he done so, he might have caught Amnon suddenly looking a great deal more cheerful.

Tamar answered her father's summons as soon as his word reached her, and she bowed low before the king on entering his quarters.

'Go to the house of your brother Amnon, who is ill and asking for you' David told her. 'Prepare some food for him and make sure he eats it'

So Tamar took some dough and herbs and hurried to do her father's bidding.

She found her half brother lying on his bed and set to work at once to knead the dough and make the bread in his sight. Then she went into the kitchen to bake it.

When she returned with the dish and offered him the bread, he refused to eat it.

'Send everyone out of here' he ordered. So all the attendants left the room leaving them alone together.

'Bring the bread here' Amnon said, 'so that I may eat from your hand'

'What a baby!' Tamar teased. 'All right.'

She knelt beside the bed smiling, but he reached out his hand and grasped her wrist, making her drop the bread.

'Oh!'

Tamar made to pick up the bread with her other hand, but he dragged her closer.

'Never mind the bread. Come, lie with me here, that we may enjoy each other.'

'No!' She tried to break free, but he was too strong and now sat up. 'Don't force me', she begged. 'Such an evil thing should not be done in Israel'

But Amnon laughed. 'Tell that to the king. Have you not heard how he took Bathsheba?!

'What about me, then; how could I get rid of my disgrace?'

But Amnon pulled her roughly onto the bed beside him and grasped her more firmly in his arms.

'Please, speak to the king, Tamar begged 'He will not keep me from being married to you. please!'

But Amnon would not listen and because he was stronger than she, tore the robe from her and forced himself into her.

Afterwards he stood up and looked down at Tamar, who was weeping, and suddenly he hated her. He could have had any woman. What on earth had possessed him to take her—lying there, snivelling like a child?

'Get up,' he snarled, 'and get out'.

'No!' Tamar sat up, trying to pull the robe around her shoulders, which were bruised where his hands had grasped her. 'Sending me away now would be a greater wrong than what you have already done to me'.

But Amnon refused to listen and opening the door, called his personal servant and ordered: 'Get this woman out of the house and bolt the door behind her'.

So Tamar went away weeping aloud as she went.

When she arrived home, Absolom her brother came out to meet her and took her into his arms to comfort her.

'Has Amnon your brother been with you?'

Tamar nodded and burst into fresh tears. But after a while, Absolom said, 'Be quiet now, my sister. He is your brother. Don't take this to heart'.

But Tamar lived with her brother from then on, a desolate woman.

When the king heard about this, he was furious, but Absolom never said a word about it to Amnon either good or bad. But from then on, he hated Amnon and waited for when he could avenge his sister.

Two years later, it was sheep shearing time and Absolom and his men gathered his flocks at a place near the border with the tribe of Ephraim. And because it had been a bumper harvest, Absalom sent word to the King and invited him to come with his officials for the celebration. But the King replied:

'No, my son. we are too many and will be a burden to you.' And although Absolom sent another message asking David to reconsider, he still refused, but gave him his blessing.

Then Absolom arrived at the palace in person and asked. 'If the king himself will not come, then let his eldest son come in his place'

So eventually, the king agreed and sent Amnon with the rest of his grown up sons to the feast.

Absolom instructed his men: 'Listen, at the celebration, when Amnon is in high spirits from drinking and I say to you 'strike!' Then strike Amnon down and kill him. Don't be afraid. Be strong and brave, for this is my responsibility and I will answer to the king for it.'

So when Amnon had drunk his fill, Absalom ordered his men to strike him down, and they did so, and he died.

Then all the king's other sons rose from the tables in fear, mounted their mules and fled.

While they were on their way, a report of what had happened reached David: 'Absolom has struck down all the king's sons. Not none of them is left!

The King stood up and tore his clothes. But Jonadab, friend of Amnon, who had never doubted that Absolom would revenge himself one day said: 'My lord should not think that all the princes are dead, but only Amnon, I am sure.'

'How can you be sure?' David demanded. But Jonadab did not need to give an answer for the sound of shouting from the courtyard below answered for him and soon all the king's sons burst into the room and were embraced by their father. And they wept for Amnon.

At day break, the King sent soldiers to escort Absolom back to Jerusalem, but on arrival they discovered he had fled.

Absalom went to Ammihud, king of the neighbouring land of Geshur and stayed there for three years.

Eventually, time softened David's grief for Amnon and he longed to see his second son once more. But this was something he scarcely knew how to admit, even to himself.

Joab learned of this, and after giving the matter some thought sent for a wise woman he knew and could trust from the town of Teoka.

When she was rested from the journey, he had her brought to him.

'I want you to do me a service', he told her.

The old woman bowed low as Joab continued: 'I want you to seek an audience with the king.'

'The king! Surely my Lord has ready access to his Majesty?'

'But listen . . . . and do not be afraid of what I am going to ask you, because the king himself will reward you. First, you must pretend that you are in mourning'

With Joab's help, the old woman was amongst those given a place the following morning with those permitted to present a petition to the king When it was her turn, she shuffled forward, then fell with her face to the ground to pay him honour.

'Help me O king' she cried.

'What is it you want?' David answered, and the old woman raised her head.

'I am indeed a widow,' she began, 'but I your servant had two sons. They got into a fight and no one was able to separate them. Then one struck the other and killed him.'

David nodded sympathetically. 'That is a great sorrow. But what can I do? Even a king has no power over death.'

'My whole clan has risen up against me. They say 'hand over the one who struck down his brother so that we may put him to death for the life of the one he killed.' They would put out the only burning coal I have left, leaving my husband without name or descent on the face of the earth!'

Then David said 'Stand up and go home. I will issue an order on your behalf'. If anyone says anything more concerning this matter, bring him to me. Not a hair of your son's head will fall to the ground'.

The woman bowed again then she said: 'Please let your servant speak once more to the king'.

'Speak', David told her.

'When the king says this, does he not convict himself?

'Explain yourself' David said frowning.

The old woman trembled, but remembering Joab's words she continued: 'The king has not brought back his banished son. Like water spilled on the ground which cannot be recovered, so we must die. But God does not take away life; instead, he devises ways so that a banished person may not remain estranged from him. And now I have come to say this, as the king would do for me, may he not do also for himself and his own son? And may the Lord your God be with you.'

David rose from his judgement seat and again the woman fell with her face to the ground.

'Isn't the hand of Joab in this?' he demanded.

The woman raised her head and glanced for a moment at Joab himself who had been standing to one side listening to this before turning back to the king.

'My lord has wisdom like that of an angel—he knows everything that happens in the land. Yes, it was your servant, my lord Joab, who instructed me to speak—to change the present situation.'

'I see' The King turned to Joab. 'And what has my lord Joab got to say?

Joab came forward, and knelt before David.

'What the woman says is true, my Lord. The people long to see the king reconciled with his eldest son'.

David paused for a moment, then he reached out his hand.' I must be more stubborn than I thought to require such play acting!'

Joab rose to his feet, and taking the king's hand, bent down and kissed it.

'Sometimes others know us where we know not ourselves', he murmured.

David nodded.

'Very well, go and bring back the young man, Absalom.

Chapter fifteen

The following day, Joab set out for Geshur with an escort to bring back Absolom, but the king ordered that he must go to his own house and not come to the palace until sent for.

In all Israel there was no one so highly praised for his handsome appearance as Absolom. From the top of his head to the soles of his feet there was no blemish in him.

Three sons and a daughter were born to him. He named the daughter after his sister Tamar and she too became a beautiful woman.

Absalom lived for two years without seeing the king's face. Then he sent for Joab, but he too refused to see him He sent for him a second time, but again Joab refused. So losing patience Absolom said to his servants: 'Look, Joab's barley field is next to mine, go and set it on fire.' The servants looked at each other anxiously but they did as he commanded, and it did produce the desired effect.

Infuriated, Joab stormed into Absalom's house and demanded to know why he had ordered his servants to do such a thing. But Absalom looked at him coolly

'I asked you to visit me so I could send word to the king. He rose to his feet to face Joab. 'why have I come back from

Geshur? It would be better if I were still there!. I want to see my fatherr's face, and if I am guilty of anything, let him put me to death'.

Despite himself, Joab had to suppress a smile. The resemblance to David, not so much in appearance, but in manner reminded him so much of David when they were young outlaws together. It was uncanny and he found the anger with which he had entered the house evaporate.

'Very well. I will speak to the king' Joab managed to maintain a neutral expression, but as he turned to leave, the younger man reached out and clasped his arm.

'I won't forget this when I come to the throne' he said softly and for a moment the two looked at each other. Then Joab nodded and turned on his heel.

Absolom watched him go thoughtfully. One of the things he had inherited from his father was the ability to inspire loyalty in others. But he was not such a judge of character, and in the case of Joab, one day this was to prove fatal.

In the mean time Joab went to the king who needed little persuasion and within a few days Absolom was called to the palace.

When he came into the king's presence, he bowed with his face to the ground.

But David rose from his seat and took his son into his arms and kissed him.

Now, basking in the king's approval, Absolom started the conspiracy which was to split the royal house in two and so fulfil the prophesy made by Nathan many years since but largely forgotten And although determined, he was patient and moved to build up his position in such a way that David had no idea of his intentions until it was too late. In the mean time, he maintained all outward appearance of devotion and loyalty.

As the eldest son, he sat at the king's right hand in the Council and often represented him in entertaining the foreign dignitaries who frequently visited Jerusalem to seek David's help. Absolom also went out of his way to be pleasant and courteous to David's wives as well as his own mother and to indulge his younger brothers, particularly Solomon whom he taught to hunt with bow and spear.

He provided himself with a chariot and horses and with fifty men to run ahead of him.

He would get up early and stand by the side of the road leading to the main gate of the city, and whenever anyone came with a complaint to be placed before the king for a decision, Absalom would call out to him; 'What town are you from?' and would commiserate with him as the petitioner unburdened himself. Then he would put his arm around the man's shoulder and say: 'Look, it seems to me your claims are valid and proper, but there are many who have been waiting to be heard for days. If only I were appointed judge in the land, then everyone who had a complaint could come to me and I would see he received justice'. And whenever anyone approached to bow down before him, Absalom would reach out his hand and take hold of him to embrace him.

He behaved in this way to all the Israelites who came to the king asking for justice, and so he stole away the hearts of many.

At the end of four years, Absolom said to the king: 'Let me go to our home town of Hebron and fulfil a vow I made to the Lord while I was living in Geshur. I vowed that if the Lord took me back to Jerusalem I will worship him there'

The king smiled and said: 'It will be good to visit our clan while many still live. I wish I could come with you, but go in peace'.

When he reached Hebron, Absolom sent messengers and heralds secretly throughout the tribes of Israel to proclaim: 'When you hear the sound of trumpets, shout 'Absolom is king in Hebron'.

Two hundred and fifty men from Jerusalem accompanied Absolom to Hebron. They had been invited as guests and most had gone quite innocently, knowing nothing of this.

While he was offering sacrifices with a great show of piety, Absalom also sent for Ahithopel, one of his father's chief councillors to come from his home town of Giloh, which was nearby. And so the conspiracy gained strength and Absolom's following kept on increasing.

By the time news of this reached the king a great number of men, who had either not known him or retained secret resentment on account of his taking the crown from the house of Saul, had already rallied to Absalom and had been organised into a formidable army.

David said to all the officials who were with him: 'Come, we must escape or we shall be trapped here in Jerusalem. We must leave immediately or Absalom will overtake us and put both the city and we ourselves to the sword'.

Joab and his brother Abishai argued to begin with that they should stay and fight the rebel army 'for surely the Lord will give them into our hands?'

'And so he may' David answered, 'at the appointed time. But we can organise our defence more surely away from the confines of the city and gain time for those loyal to us to come to our aid'.

And so the king set out with his entire household, but he left ten concubines to take care of the palace. They halted at an agreed place some distance away and here Joab, Abishai and all the fighting men loyal to him joined him including the six hundred Gittites who had come with him from Gath before he became king so many years ago. Some of these were well beyond the normal age to bear arms, but they had rallied to the king without exception.

Deeply moved, David said to Ittal their leader.: 'Why should you come along with us? You are an exile from your homeland. Go back and serve king Absolom. Should I make you wander about with us when I don't yet know the Lord's will? Go back, and take your countrymen with you, and may kindness and faithfulness be with you'.

But Ittal answered: 'As surely as the Lord lives, and as my lord the king lives, wherever the king may be, whether in life or death, there will your servants be.'

So David embraced him, and said: 'Very well. Go ahead; march on.'

So Ittal resumed his place at the head of his men and all their families, and marched ahead with all David's other soldiers and their families.

As they travelled along, it seemed the whole countryside turned out to see the king pass by and many wept aloud as he moved on towards the desert.

Zadok, one of the chief priests was there with the other Levites who carried with them the Ark of the Covenant as was Abiathar, the priest who had been with David since he had fled from Saul. He had waited at the gate of the city until the last who wanted to leave had done so safely.

But David said to Zadok: 'Take the Ark back into the city. If I find favour in the Lord's eyes, he will bring me back and let me see his dwelling place again. But if he is not pleased with me, then I am ready; let him do to me whatever seems good to him. Go in peace with Abiathar, and take your son Ahimaz, and Jonathan, son of Abiathar, but keep your ears and eyes open. We will wait at the Jordan river until we hear from you.'

Zadok nodded. And the two priests went back to the city with their sons.

Shortly afterwards David found Hushai, one of his chief advisors waiting along the road to join them, but again David said to him: 'My old friend, you have given me many years of loyal service, but now If you come with me you will be a burden to both of us. You can serve me best by returning with Zadok

But your majesty . . ' the old man began, but David held up his hand and Hushai saw a glint of purpose in his master's eyes.

'Say to Absolom, I will be your servant O King. I was your father's servant in the past but now I will be your servant. 'The king allowed himself a grim smile. 'And even if he has doubts to begin with, you are the most highly regarded of all my councillors and he will be flattered that you should be willing to accept him in my place. Then you can help me by confusing the advice he gets from others.'

Hushai nodded gravely and bowed before turning to go. Then David called after him.

'The priests Zadok and Abiathar will be there. Tell them anything you hear in the palace. Their two sons are there with them and will be sent to me.'

After Absalom and all the men with him arrived in Jerusalem, Hushai went to him and greeted him: 'Long live the king! Long live the king!'

But Absalom frowned: 'Is this the way you show love to your friend? Why didn't you go with him?'

Hushai answered: 'The one chosen by the Lord as punishment for your father's sin in taking the wife of Uriah and causing his death; the one chosen by those here and all the men of Israel—his I will be.'

Absalom paused for a moment then he nodded and turned to his advisors.

'Give us your advice. What should we do?'

Ahitopel stepped forward.

'Lie with your father's concubines whom he left to take care of the palace' he said. 'Then all Israel will hear that you have made yourself an offence to your father in defiance of him, and all with you will be encouraged!'

So they pitched a tent on the palace roof and all the concubines were led to Absalom and he ravaged them in the sight of everyone.

Then Ahitophel said: 'Now I would choose twelve thousand of your most experienced soldiers and set out tonight in pursuit of David and attack him before he reaches the Jordan, and while he is tired as well as those with him. I would strike him down, but only the king. Then bring all the rest back with you unharmed.

This advice seemed good to Absolom and all his other advisors. But then Absolom turned back to the new arrival and said,' and what do you advise?'

Ahitophel and the others glanced at each other worriedly, as well they might for Hushai immediately said: 'The advice Ahitophel has given this time is not good'.

Ahitophel began to protest, but Absalom held up his hand to silence him, and Hushai continued:

'You know your father and his men; they are fighters, and will be as fierce as a wild bear robbed of her cubs. Besides, your father is wily and will not spend the night with his troops. Even now, he is hidden in a cave or some other place. And if he should attack your troops when they least expect it, as he has surprised his enemies so often in the past, and overwhelm them, the story will become known that there has been a great slaughter among the troops who follow Absolom. Then even your bravest soldier will melt with fear for everyone knows that your father is the most experienced fighter in all Israel and that those with him are the bravest. So I advise you, let all Israel from Dan to Beersheba—as numerous as the sand on the sea shore—be gathered to you, with you yourself leading them into battle. Then we will attack him wherever he may be found, and we will fall on him as the dew settles on the ground. Neither he, nor any of his men will be left alive.'

Absolom and all his advisors besides Ahitophel agreed that this advice was better, for the Lord had determined to frustrate the good advice of Ahitophel to bring disaster on Absolom.

Hushai lost no time in telling Zadok what had taken place and they agreed to send a message immediately to David. 'Do not stay at the Jordan but cross over immediately or the king and all the people with him will be swallowed up!'.

Jonathan and Ahimaaz, the priests' sons had been staying at a village close to Jerusalem. A servant girl was to go and give them any message for David as they could not risk being seen entering the city. But a young man saw them with her and reported this to an official at the palace. Hearing of this, the two young men hid at a friend's house. He had a well in his garden and they climbed into it. Then the wife took a covering and spread it over the well and scattered grain over it for the hens. When Absalom's men searched the district she said to them she had seen the priests' sons but they had crossed the nearby brook in the direction of En Rogel. So the Guard searched but found no one and returned to Jerusalem. As soon as they had gone, Jonathan and Ahimaz came up out of the well and hurried to catch up with the king to give him the news the girl had brought.

Acting on this, David and those with him crossed the Jordan and found refuge in the small town of Mahanaim. They were exhausted, but it took several days for Absalom to gather his forces and in the mean time many of David's wealthy friends brought him bedding and supplies. Thus encouraged, David sent out messengers throughout Israel and many of his best fighting men flocked to join him.

David mustered these and appointed commanders of hundreds and commanders of thousands. Thus organised, he divided the army into three divisions: a third under Joab, a third under his brother Abishai and a third under Ittai, the Gittite.

David told the troops 'I myself will march out with you'. But the men said, 'You must not go out. If we are forced to flee, they won't care about us. Even if half of us die, they won't care; but you are worth ten thousand of us. It would be better for you to give us support from the city'.

Greatly moved, David answered: 'I will do whatever seems best to you'.

So the king stood beside the gate while all the men marched out in their divisions. But he commanded Joab, Abishai and Ittai 'Be gentle with the young man Absalom for my sake'. And all the troops heard this.

David's army marched to meet the army of his son, Absolom. The battle was joined in the Forest of Ephraim. Absolom's soldiers were more numerous than those of David, but David's commanders were far more experienced and by deft manoeuvres cut the opposing force into isolated units and slaughtered them.—over twenty thousand in all. The battle spread out over the whole countryside and wild animals in the forest-lions and snakes claimed as many lives as the sword.

When he saw the battle was lost, Absolom deserted his troops and fled on his mule, but as it passed under some trees

Absalom's head got caught in the branch of a tree and he was left hanging as the mule galloped away.

At that moment, a number of Joab's soldiers who had been sent after him arrived and saw what had happened. At once an argument broke out between those who wanted the honour of killing him and those who had heard the king's words. So one was sent to fetch Joab, who only glanced briefly at the helpless prince when he arrived before demanding angrily why the rebel still lived.

'I would have given you ten shekels of silver and a warriors belt' he told them. But one braver than the rest replied: 'Even if a thousand shekels were weighed out in front of me, I would not lift my hand against the king's son. I heard the king say to you 'protect the young man Absolom for my sake.'

Joab, snorted, and pushing the upstart impatiently to one side, rode to where Absalom was still hanging, guarded by the rest of those who had found him.

Dismounting, Jaob drew a short javelin from the horses saddle, and without hesitating, plunged it into Absalom's body. Then, seeing Absalom was still alive, he waived forward his body guard and they surrounded him and killed him with their swords. Then they took down his body and threw it into a hole in the ground and piled rocks on top of it.

Then Jaob ordered a trumpet to be sounded and David's army stopped pursuing what was left of Absalom's army and allowed them to flee to their homes.

When the king heard of his son's death he was shaken and went up to his room which was over the gateway and wept. Joab was told the king was weeping for his son, and for the whole army the victory was turned into mourning and the men stole back into the city that evening as men who are ashamed when they flee from battle.

Infuriated, Joab went up to the king's quarters and spoke more harshly than he had ever dared to before.

'Today you have humiliated all your men, who have just saved your life and the lives of your wives and your sons and daughters' he shouted.

David raised his head and looked at him as the other continued: 'You have made it clear that the commanders and their men mean nothing to you. That you would be pleased if Absalom were alive today and all the rest of us were dead!'

'No . . .' the king rose to his feet to face his accuser, but before he could say anything Joab went on:

'Then go out and encourage your men or I swear by the Lord that if you don't, not a man will be left with you by nightfall and this will be worse than all the calamities that have fallen on you from your youth until now'

The two men stared at each other, then the king nodded.

'And would that include you and Abishai?' he asked softly.

After a moment, Joab allowed himself a grim smile.

'You'll never know, will you?'

But David heeded his advice took his seat in the gateway of the city with his wives and children behind him. And when the men were told, 'the king is sitting in the gateway', they all gathered in front of him and cheered.

Chapter sixteen

Their fellow countrymen who had fled to their homes began to argue among themselves.

'The king delivered us from the hand of all our enemies' many said. 'He is the one who rescued us from the Philistines, but now he has fled the country because of Absolom. But he whom we anointed to rule over us is dead, so why do you say nothing about bringing the king back?'.

Word of this reached David so he sent a message to Zadok and Abaithar.

'Ask the elders of Judah, my own tribe, 'Why should you be the last to bring the king back to his palace since what is being said throughout Israel has reached my ears.'

So David won back the hearts of all the men of Judah including Amasa, Judah's foremost warrior, whom David swore to appoint head of all the army in place of Joab. They sent word begging him to return, and at an appointed time assembled as one man on the banks of the Jordan river to escort him back to Jerusalem.

When they heard what was planned, the troops of Israel's other tribes hurried down to join them and so the king returned with great rejoicing.

But no longer had this taken place than a man called Sheba, of the tribe of Benjamin, the tribe of king Saul, raised a rebellion and persuaded some of those who had supported Absolom to desert. So David sent a message to Amasa and commanded him to summon the men of Judah and come with them to Jerusalem within three days.

But while he went to follow the king's orders, Amasa took longer than three days and David said to Abishai: 'Now Sheba will do us more harm than Absalom ever did. Take your brother's men and pursue him or he will escape from us'

Abishai gathered together Joab's men, including Joab himself, who was well aware of the reason David had by-passed him a second time.

Just after they reached Gibeon, Amasa caught up with them, but before Abishai could stop him, Joab walked back to meet him smiling and said, 'And how are you, my brother?' and taking Amasa's hand reached forward as if to greet him, but slipped his dagger out of its sheath with his other hand and plunged it into the newcomer's heart so he fell down dead. Then one of Joab's men stood beside the body and called out to those who had been following Amasa: 'Whoever favours Joab and whoever is for David, let them follow Joab'

Amasa's body lay in the middle of the road wallowing in blood and his men came to a halt when they reached it, so the man who had called out to them dragged it to the side and threw a garment over it Then all of them fell in beside those of Joab and they continued on together.

Sheba finally took refuge in a city in the far north called Beth Maach. All Joab's men and those who had joined them began to build siege ramps. But an old wise woman called down to them from the walls and asked them to bring Joab so she could speak to him.

When he appeared she called down: 'Are you Joab?'

'I am'.

'Then listen to what your servant has to say'

'I'm listening' Joab assured her'

'Well, long ago when anyone had a problem, they used to say they could always find an answer here in Beth Maach.'

'Go on'.

'We are a peaceful and loyal city that is like a mother in Israel. Why do you want to swallow us up?'

'Far be it from me to do such a thing' Joab called back. 'That is not the case. But you are sheltering a man called Sheba from the hill country of Ephraim who has lifted up his hand against king David. Hand over this one man and we will withdraw from the city'

The woman nodded, then she said: 'His head will be thrown to you from the wall'.

She went to the elders of the city who listened to her advice and agreed to cut off the head of Sheba. And so it was thrown to Joab from the wall.

So Joab ordered a trumpet to be sounded and his men withdrew from the city, each returning to his home, while Joab and Abishai returned to Jerusalem.

There were then no more serious challenges to David's rule, although in time he was compelled by advancing years to let others fight his battles for him. He lived many years to enjoy his music and his family, particularly Solomon his youngest son And when occasionally he thought about it, David hoped that the prophesy made so long ago by Nathan that 'a sword would never be far from those he loved' had been fulfilled through the suffering inflicted by Absalom.

He composed many songs for voice and harp, one of the best loved he played for the first time to his family one quiet evening in late summer towards the end of his life. This was recorded by a young musician of the court whose name has long been forgotten, but not the song itself:

> *The Lord is my rock, my fortress and my deliverer*
> *My God is my rock in whom I take shelter*
> *My shield and the sword of my salvation*
> *From violent men he saves me*
> *I call to the Lord, who is worthy of praise and I am*
> *saved from my enemies.*

When the sound of the harp died away there was a moment's silence. Then Abigail, no longer young herself, who was sitting close to him lent forward and squeezed his hand. Their eyes met and they both smiled.

Over the years, David became known as 'the sweet singer of Israel.'

When he was old, he found he could not keep warm, even when they put covers over him. So his servants said to him: 'Let us find a young virgin to attend the king and take care of him. She can lie beside him so that our lord may keep warm.' So they searched throughout Israel for a beautiful girl and found Aisha and brought her to him.

She was gentle and very beautiful. she took care of the king and waited on him, but he had no intimate relations with her.

About this time, Adonijah, the king's eldest surviving son, put himself forward boasting: 'I will soon be king'.

He got chariots and horses ready with fifty men to run ahead of him. But his father never challenged him although the similarity to the behaviour of Absalom all those years ago filled him with apprehension. But this time it was not the king himself who was threatened.

Adonijah conferred with Joab and with Abithar the priest and they gave him their support. But Zadok, Benaiah, commander of David's bodyguard, Nathan the prophet and David's special guards did not join Adonijah.

Adonijah prepared a feast. He invited all the king's sons and all the men of Judah who were royal officials, but he did not invite those who had refused to support him, nor did he ask his brother Solomon.

Nathan went to Bathsheba, Solomon's mother, and said to her: 'Haven't you heard that Adonijah has become king without our lord David knowing?'

Bathsheba looked at him in alarm. 'He hates Solomon' she said fearfully. 'He will have him killed; and me too probably!'

The Prophet nodded. 'Then let me tell you how you can save his life as well as your own. Go into the king and say to him,' My Lord, did you not swear to me that Solomon will be king after you and sit on the royal throne? Why then has Adonijah become king?' And while you are still there talking to him, I will come in and confirm what you have said'.

David was furious when he heard what Bathsheba and Nathan had to say but realised that, despite his hopes, if he did not move swiftly and with care, the sword that had lain dormant since the death of Absolom would once more bring destruction to the family.

Gathering his strength, he summoned two chariots, one for himself to be driven by Benaiah and one for Solomon.

Closely followed by Zadok, Nathan and his bodyguard, the king was driven to the place where the brook of Gihon emerged from the cave at the foot of Mount Zion on which Jerusalem was built and through which he had taken the city from the Jebusites just after he himself was crowned king of all Israel. There he dismounted and said to Solomon in a loud voice so that all those with him could hear:

'Now I will carry out the oath I swore to your mother—that you shall be king after me and sit on the throne in my place'.

At his command Solomon was anointed in the waters of the brook by Nathan, and all present bowed down and shouted 'Long live king Solomon'

Then David said, 'Go with him back to the palace and sit him on my throne. Sound the trumpets and proclaim that I, David, have appointed him ruler over Israel and Judah.'

Benaiah said; 'Amen! As the Lord was with my lord the King, so may he be with Solomon and make his throne even greater than the throne of my lord King David'.

Then all those present escorted Solomon back to the city where the trumpets were sounded and the word spread quickly so that all the people shouted: 'Long live king Solomon'.

Still by the stream, David looked around remembering. It was fitting that this which had been his own entry into Jerusalem should be the place where his son became king.

Then he nodded and was helped into the chariot to follow the others back to the palace.

Adonijah and all the guests with him were finishing their feast. On hearing the sound of the trumpets, Joab frowned: 'What is the meaning of all the noise in the city?' he said, looking round.

'Perhaps the people are already celebrating our lord Adonijah's succession to the throne', another guest ventured.

But even as he was speaking, Jonathan, one of the sons of Abiathar arrived and Adonijah beckoned him to join them'.

'Come in' he shouted expansively. 'A worthy man like you must be bringing good news!' But Jonathan shook his head

'Not at all' he said, advancing to face him across the table. 'Our lord king David has made Solomon king. He went with Zadok, Nathan and the king's bodyguard and they have put him on David's throne. Now the whole city is cheering and shouting, long live king Solomon! That's the noise you can hear'.

Adonijah shook his head in disbelief as Jonathan continued, 'All the royal officials have come to the palace to congratulate David who has praised God for allowing his eyes to see his successor on his throne this day'.

At this, all the guests rose in alarm and disbursed, but Adonijah, in great fear of Solomon, fled to the tent of meeting where the Ark stood and took hold of the altar where, by tradition, no one could touch him.

News of this was brought to David and Solomon as they stood receiving the congratulations and homage of the people But when they heard the news everyone fell silent.

Benaiah drew his sword and fell on his knees before the two kings:

'Let me slay the traitor' he begged. I won't strike twice, for he would most surely have slain my lord, king Solomon at the first opportunity'.

David looked at his son; then he said: 'The judgement shall be yours. The first you make as king. Shall Adonijah live or die? Benaiah certainly speaks the truth.'

Solomon paused for a moment then he held out his hand bidding Benaiah to rise.

'Sheath your sword my old friend. No one shall die this day. Go to my brother and say if he shows himself my loyal friend from now on, not a hair of his head will fall to the ground. Tell him this is my promise made in the presence of my lord king David and all the people. But if he turns against me in future, he will most certainly die'

Benaiah bowed and turned to leave. As he did so, Nathan the prophet stepped forward.

'The Lord has chosen Solomon to rule over his people and to build a Temple for his name.' He then turned to Solomon. 'And now, as you have sheathed the sword today, so will the sword which has been a companion of the house of your father be sheathed as long as you keep the Lord's Covenant'

David bowed low then, after embracing his son, he turned and left him to receive the continuing adulation of the people.

David did not live long after this, but his remaining years were spent in peace, surrounded by his family. When his time came he was buried with great honour.

Despite all Solomon's wisdom, which rulers came from the ends of the earth to hear; to see for themselves the building of a magnificent temple, and the splendour and riches of his reign, none was remembered with as much affection as the 'Sweet singer of Israel'. The shepherd boy whom the Lord plucked from the pastures to save his people.

THE END

Lightning Source UK Ltd.
Milton Keynes UK
UKOW030746070612

193975UK00005B/3/P